GRAPHIC LIBRARY

GRAPHIC BIOGRAPHIES

BENEDICT ARNOLD

AMERICAN HERO AND TRAITOR

by Michael Burgan
illustrated by Terry Beatty

Consultant:
Wayne K. Bodle, PhD
Department of History
Indiana University of Pennsylvania

Capstone press
Mankato, Minnesota

D1400631

Graphic Library is published by Capstone Press,
1710 Roe Crest Drive, North Mankato, Minnesota 56003.
www.capstonepub.com

Library of Congress Cataloging-in-Publication Data
Burgan, Michael.
Benedict Arnold : American hero and traitor / by Michael Burgan; illustrated by Terry Beatty.
p. cm.—(Graphic library. Graphic biographies)
Includes bibliographical references and index.
ISBN: 978-0-7368-6854-9 (hardcover)
ISBN: 978-0-7368-7906-4 (softcover pbk.)
1. Arnold, Benedict, 1741–1801—Juvenile literature. 2. American loyalists—Biography—Juvenile literature. 3. Generals—United States—Biography—Juvenile literature. 4. United States. Continental Army—Biography—Juvenile literature. 5. United States—History—Revolution, 1775–1783—Juvenile literature. 6. Graphic novels. I. Beatty, Terry, ill. II. Title. III. Series.
E278.A7B87 2007
973.3'82092—dc22 2006027985

Summary: In graphic novel format, tells the story of Benedict Arnold's heroism and betrayal during the American Revolution.

Designers
Alison Thiele and Thomas Emery

Production Designer
Kim Brown

Colorist
Scott Larson

Editor
Martha E. H. Rustad

Editor's note: Direct quotations from primary sources are indicated by a yellow background.

Direct quotations appear on the following pages:
Page 14, from a 1777 letter from Benedict Arnold to General George Washington, as published in *The Life of Benedict Arnold: His Patriotism and His Treason* by Isaac N. Arnold (Chicago: Jansen, McClurg, and Company, 1880).
Page 22, from the Public Papers of Sir Henry Clinton at the University of Michigan, Ann Arbor, as published in *The Man in the Mirror: A Life of Benedict Arnold* by Clare Brandt (New York: Random House, 1994).
Page 26, from an account of the battle at Fort Griswold by Thomas Hertell, as published in *The Battle of Groton Heights: A Collection of Narratives, Official Reports, Records, & c., of the Storming of Fort Griswold, and the Burning of New London by British Troops, Under the Command of Brig.-Gen. Benedict Arnold, on the Sixth of September, 1781* by William Wallace Harris (New London, 1870).

Printed in the United States 3749

TABLE OF CONTENTS

CHAPTER 1 RISE OF A YOUNG PATRIOT

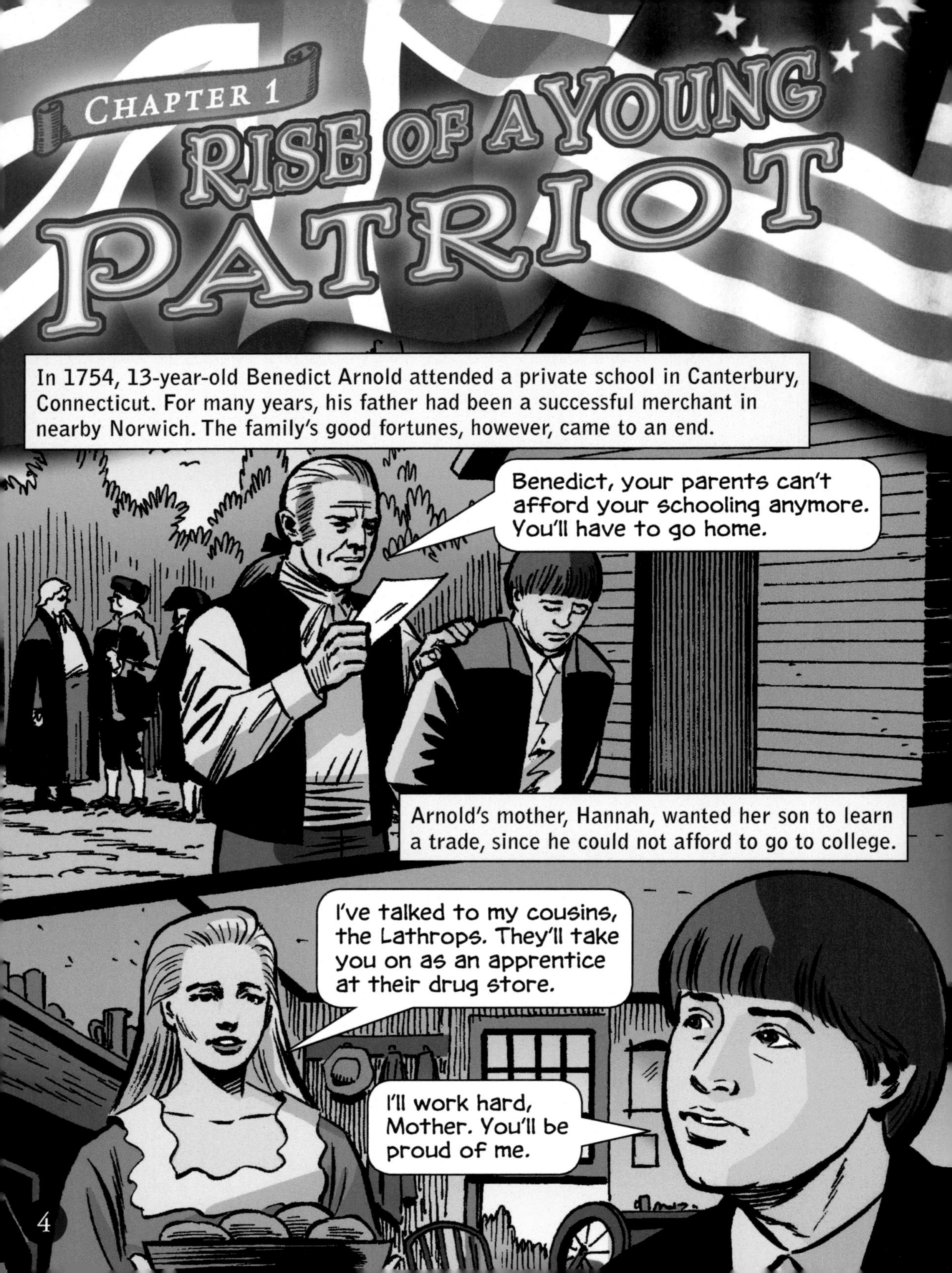

In 1754, 13-year-old Benedict Arnold attended a private school in Canterbury, Connecticut. For many years, his father had been a successful merchant in nearby Norwich. The family's good fortunes, however, came to an end.
Benedict, your parents can't afford your schooling anymore. You'll have to go home.
Arnold's mother, Hannah, wanted her son to learn a trade, since he could not afford to go to college.
I've talked to my cousins, the Lathrops. They'll take you on as an apprentice at their drug store.
I'll work hard, Mother. You'll be proud of me.

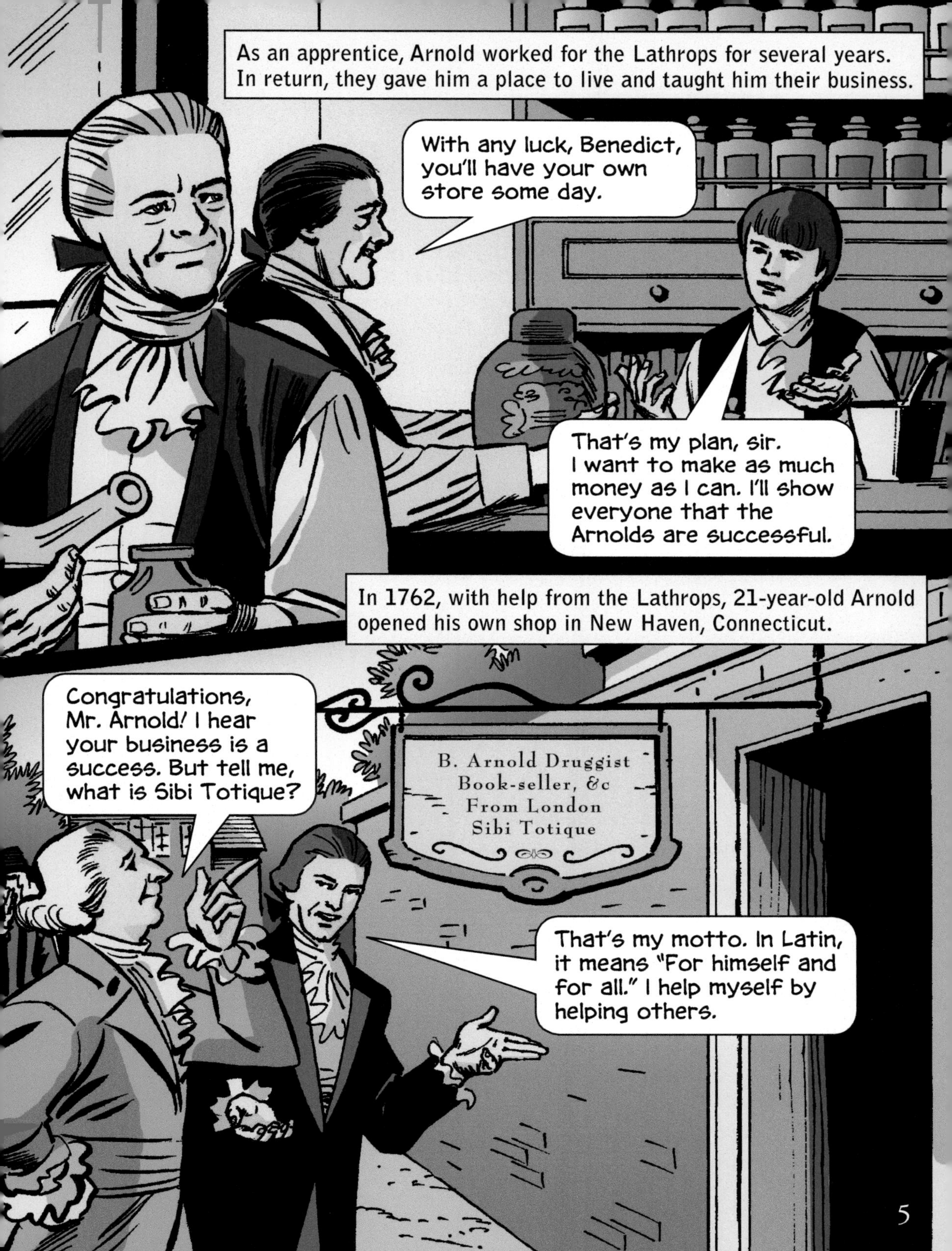
As an apprentice, Arnold worked for the Lathrops for several years. In return, they gave him a place to live and taught him their business.
With any luck, Benedict, you'll have your own store some day.
That's my plan, sir. I want to make as much money as I can. I'll show everyone that the Arnolds are successful.
In 1762, with help from the Lathrops, 21-year-old Arnold opened his own shop in New Haven, Connecticut.
Congratulations, Mr. Arnold! I hear your business is a success. But tell me, what is Sibi Totique?
B. Arnold Druggist Book-seller, &c From London Sibi Totique
That's my motto. In Latin, it means "For himself and for all." I help myself by helping others.

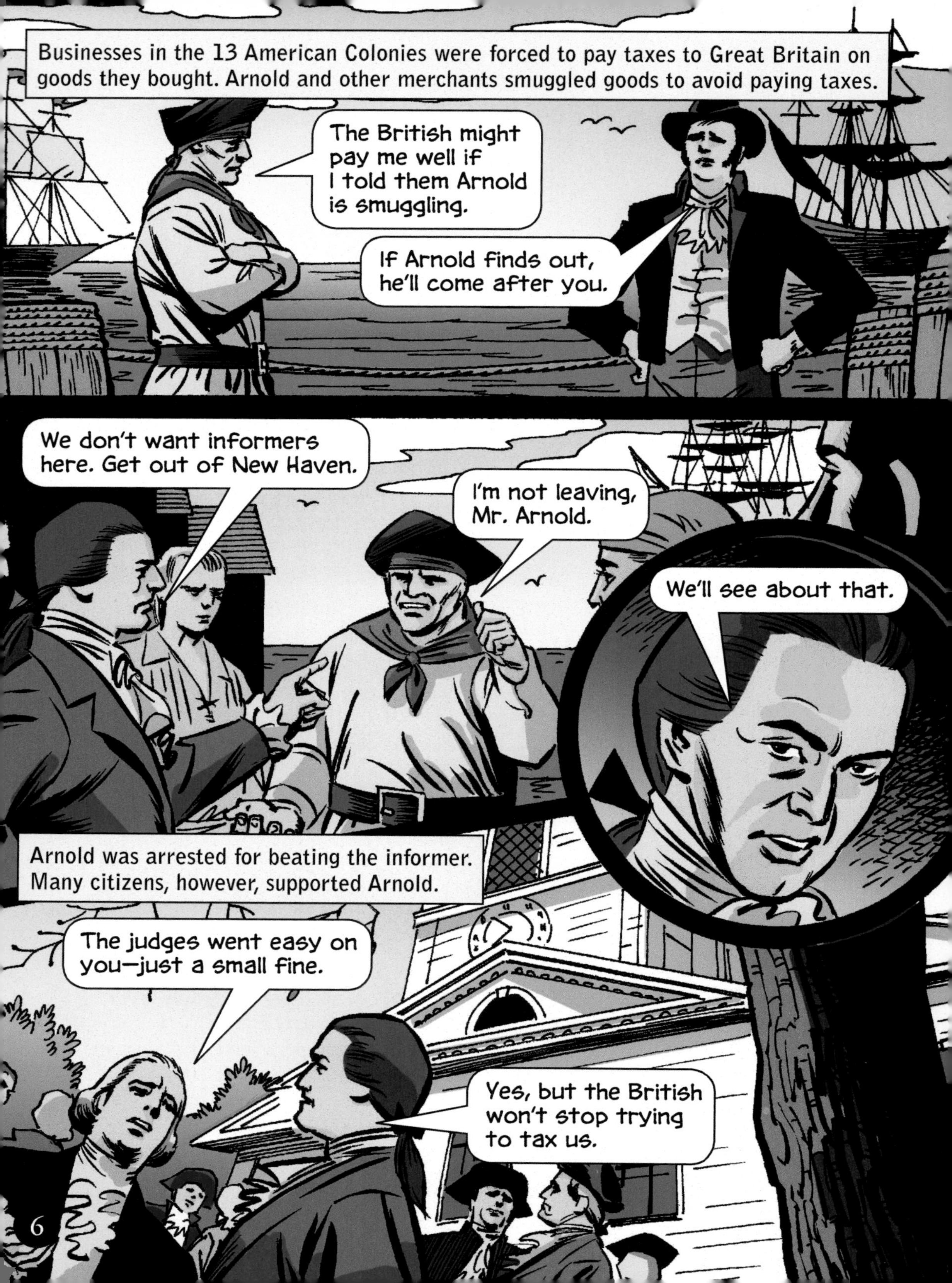
Businesses in the 13 American Colonies were forced to pay taxes to Great Britain on goods they bought. Arnold and other merchants smuggled goods to avoid paying taxes.
The British might pay me well if I told them Arnold is smuggling.
If Arnold finds out, he'll come after you.
We don't want informers here. Get out of New Haven.
I'm not leaving, Mr. Arnold.
We'll see about that.
Arnold was arrested for beating the informer. Many citizens, however, supported Arnold.
The judges went easy on you—just a small fine.
Yes, but the British won't stop trying to tax us.

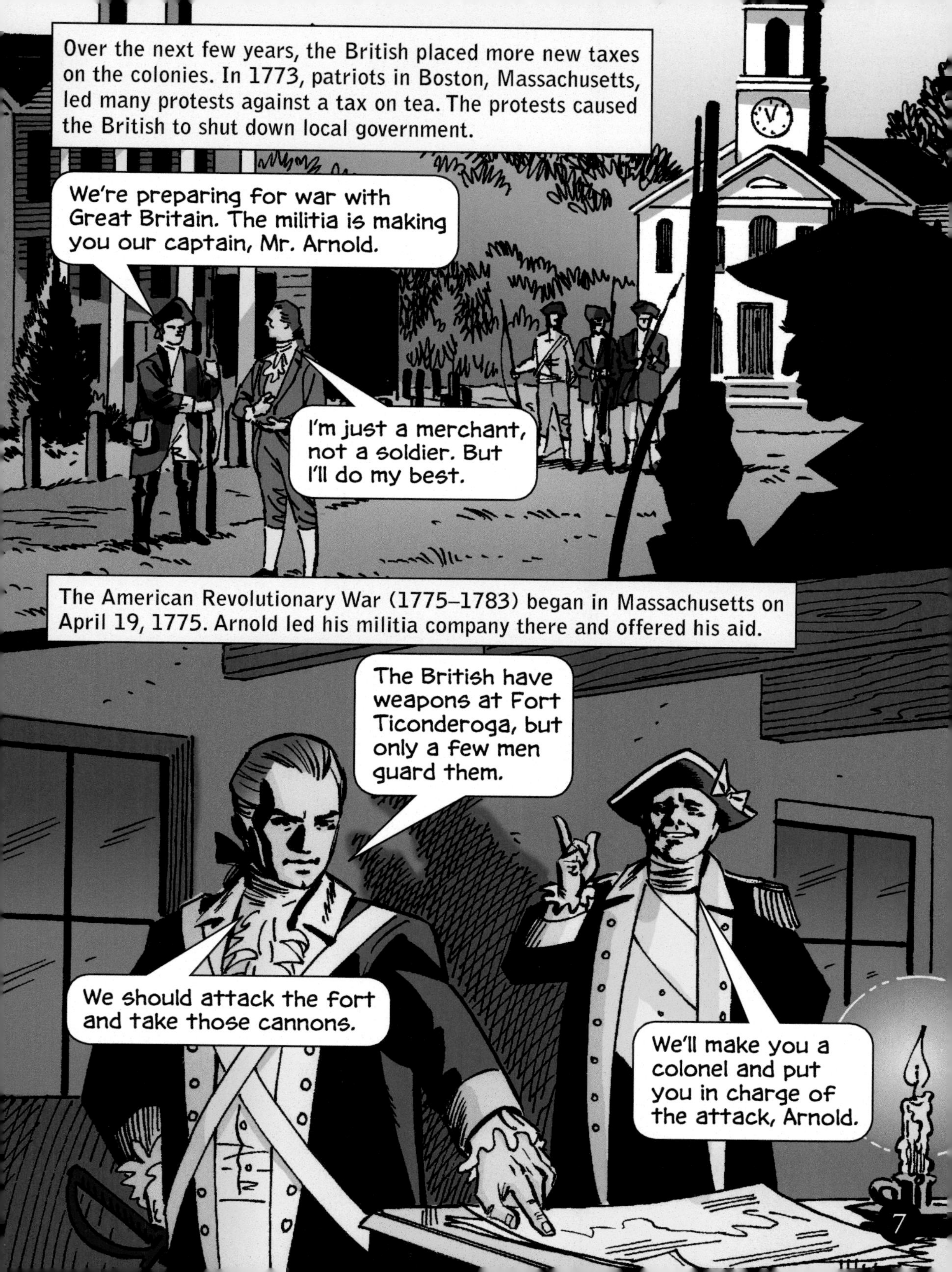
Over the next few years, the British placed more new taxes on the colonies. In 1773, patriots in Boston, Massachusetts, led many protests against a tax on tea. The protests caused the British to shut down local government.
We're preparing for war with Great Britain. The militia is making you our captain, Mr. Arnold.
I'm just a merchant, not a soldier. But I'll do my best.
The American Revolutionary War (1775–1783) began in Massachusetts on April 19, 1775. Arnold led his militia company there and offered his aid.
The British have weapons at Fort Ticonderoga, but only a few men guard them.
We should attack the fort and take those cannons.
We'll make you a colonel and put you in charge of the attack, Arnold.

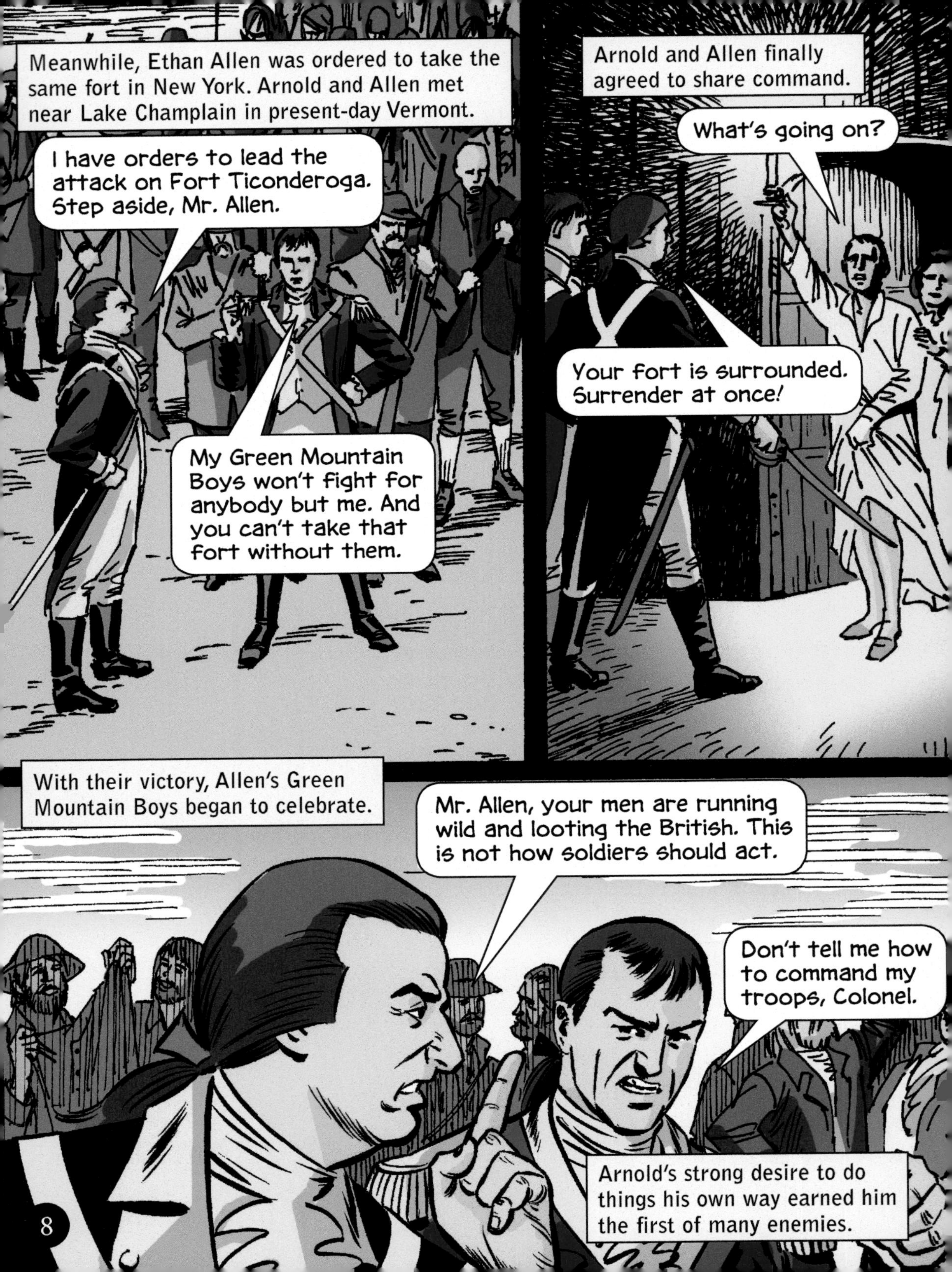
Meanwhile, Ethan Allen was ordered to take the same fort in New York. Arnold and Allen met near Lake Champlain in present-day Vermont.
I have orders to lead the attack on Fort Ticonderoga. Step aside, Mr. Allen.
My Green Mountain Boys won't fight for anybody but me. And you can't take that fort without them.
Arnold and Allen finally agreed to share command.
What's going on?
Your fort is surrounded. Surrender at once!
With their victory, Allen's Green Mountain Boys began to celebrate.
Mr. Allen, your men are running wild and looting the British. This is not how soldiers should act.
Don't tell me how to command my troops, Colonel.
Arnold's strong desire to do things his own way earned him the first of many enemies.

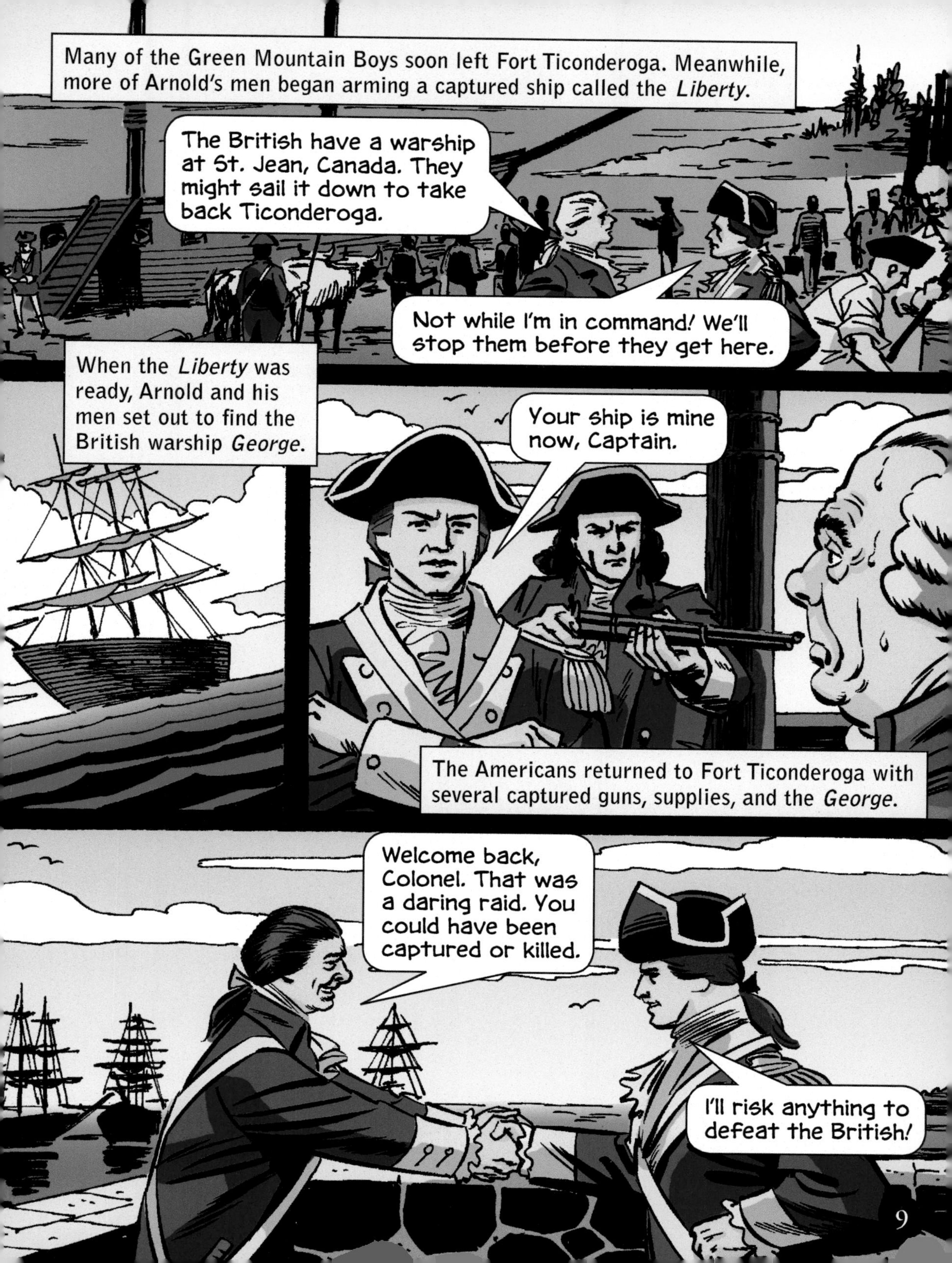
Many of the Green Mountain Boys soon left Fort Ticonderoga. Meanwhile, more of Arnold's men began arming a captured ship called the *Liberty*.
The British have a warship at St. Jean, Canada. They might sail it down to take back Ticonderoga.
Not while I'm in command! We'll stop them before they get here.
When the *Liberty* was ready, Arnold and his men set out to find the British warship *George*.
Your ship is mine now, Captain.
The Americans returned to Fort Ticonderoga with several captured guns, supplies, and the *George*.
Welcome back, Colonel. That was a daring raid. You could have been captured or killed.
I'll risk anything to defeat the British!

Chapter 2
Battlefield Hero

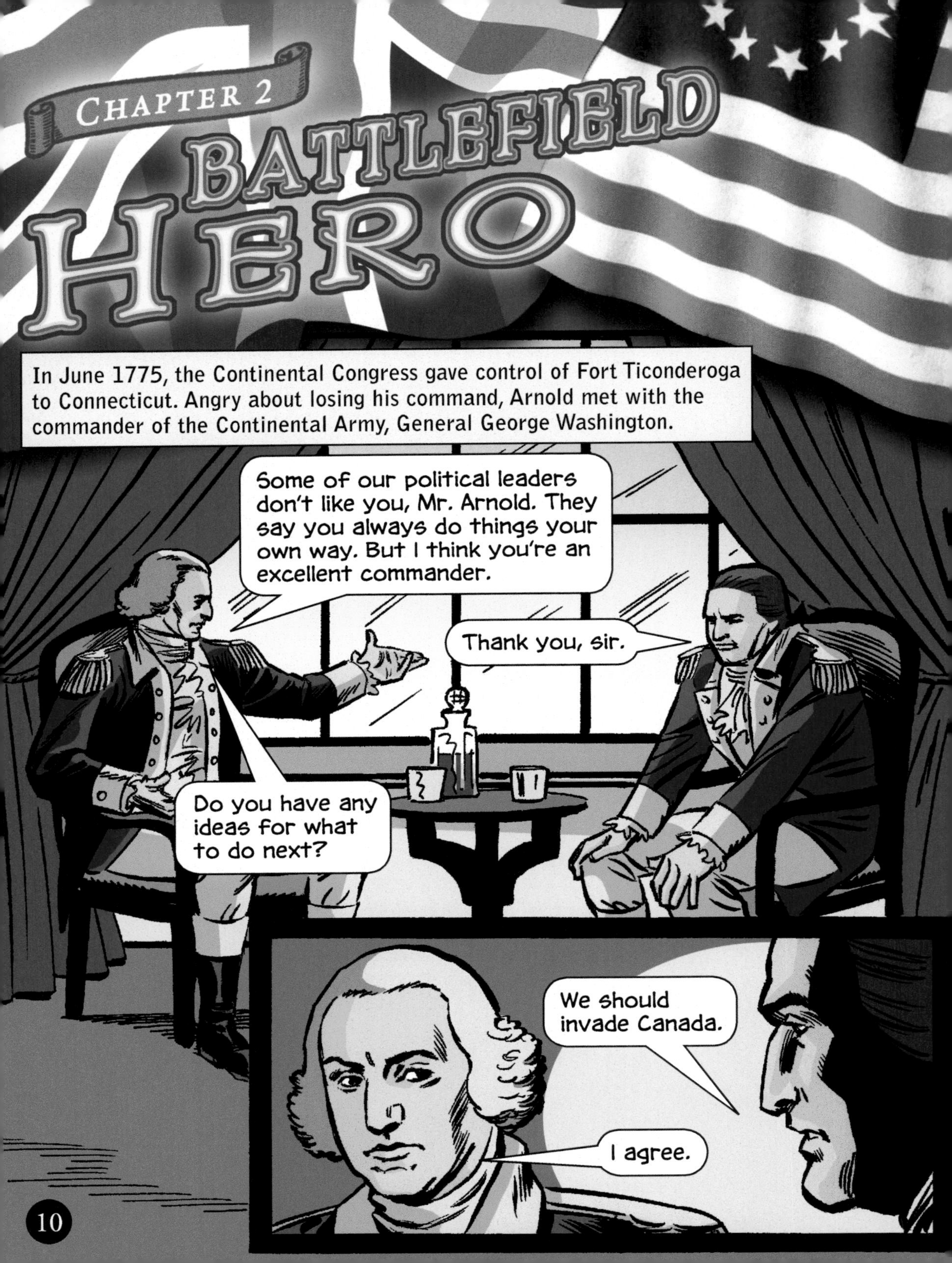
In June 1775, the Continental Congress gave control of Fort Ticonderoga to Connecticut. Angry about losing his command, Arnold met with the commander of the Continental Army, General George Washington.
Some of our political leaders don't like you, Mr. Arnold. They say you always do things your own way. But I think you're an excellent commander.
Thank you, sir.
Do you have any ideas for what to do next?
We should invade Canada.
I agree.

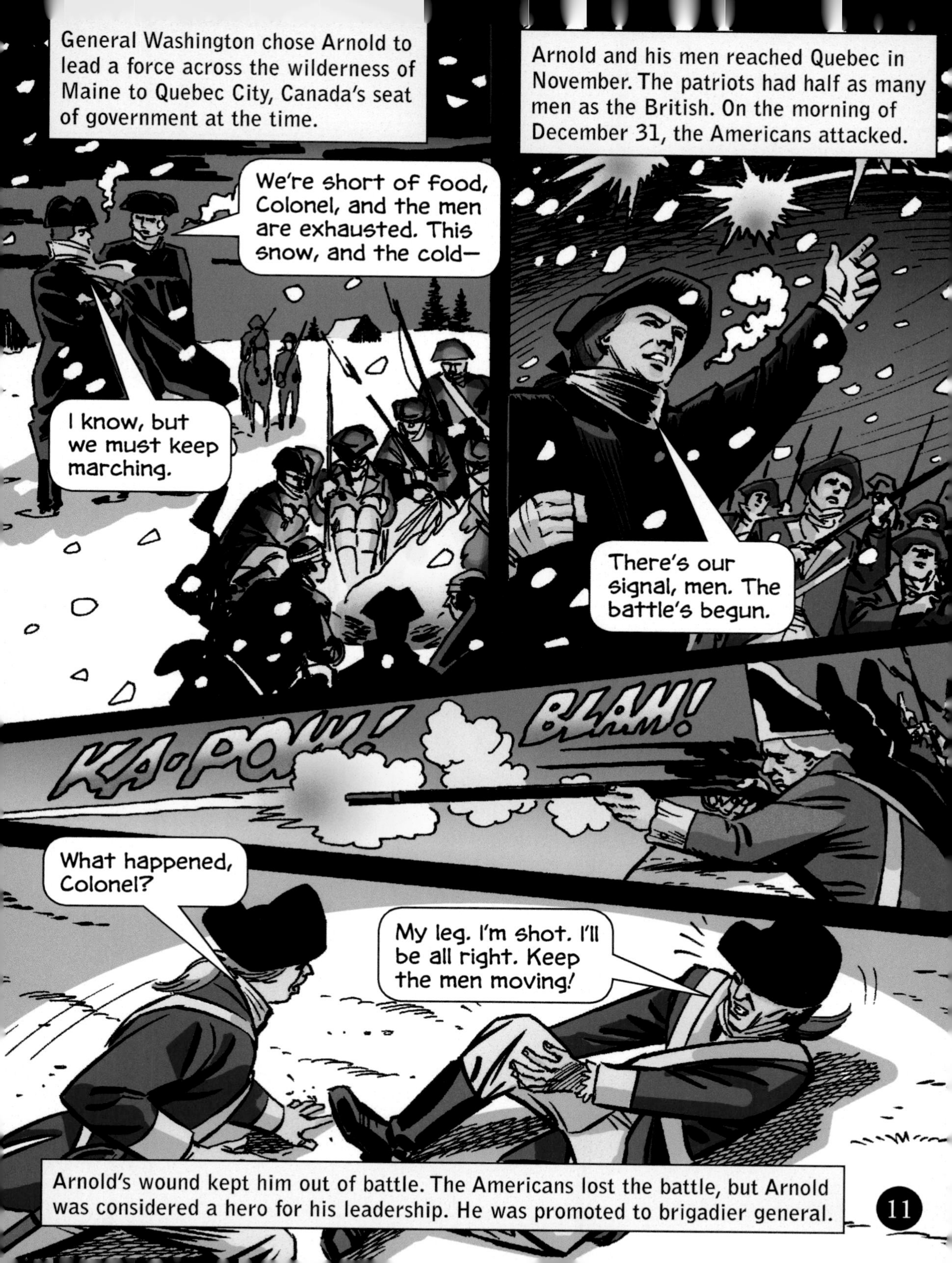
General Washington chose Arnold to lead a force across the wilderness of Maine to Quebec City, Canada's seat of government at the time.
We're short of food, Colonel, and the men are exhausted. This snow, and the cold—
I know, but we must keep marching.
Arnold and his men reached Quebec in November. The patriots had half as many men as the British. On the morning of December 31, the Americans attacked.
There's our signal, men. The battle's begun.
KA-POW!
BLAM!
What happened, Colonel?
My leg. I'm shot. I'll be all right. Keep the men moving!
Arnold's wound kept him out of battle. The Americans lost the battle, but Arnold was considered a hero for his leadership. He was promoted to brigadier general.

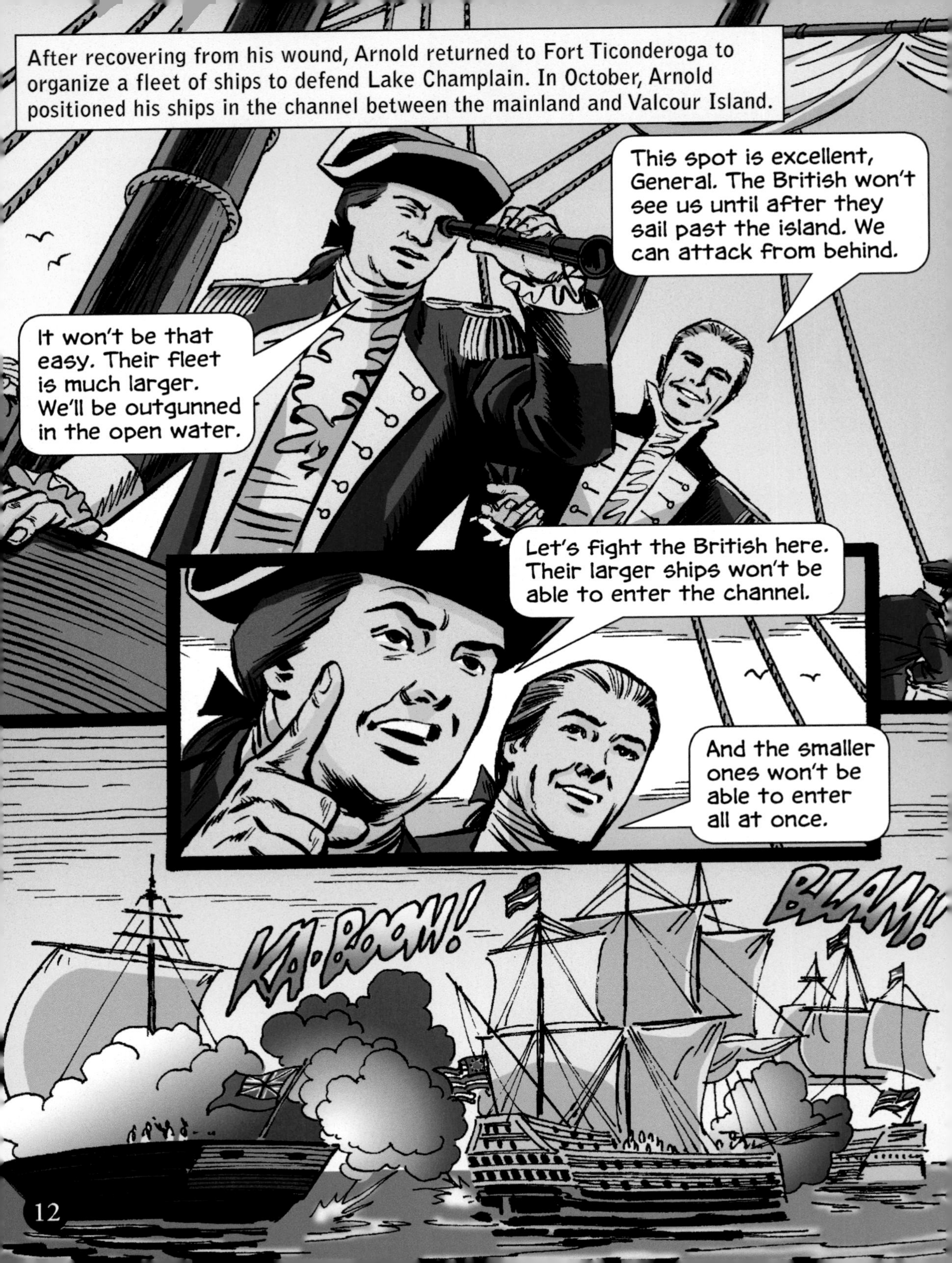
After recovering from his wound, Arnold returned to Fort Ticonderoga to organize a fleet of ships to defend Lake Champlain. In October, Arnold positioned his ships in the channel between the mainland and Valcour Island.
This spot is excellent, General. The British won't see us until after they sail past the island. We can attack from behind.
It won't be that easy. Their fleet is much larger. We'll be outgunned in the open water.
Let's fight the British here. Their larger ships won't be able to enter the channel.
And the smaller ones won't be able to enter all at once.
KA-BOOM!
BLAM!

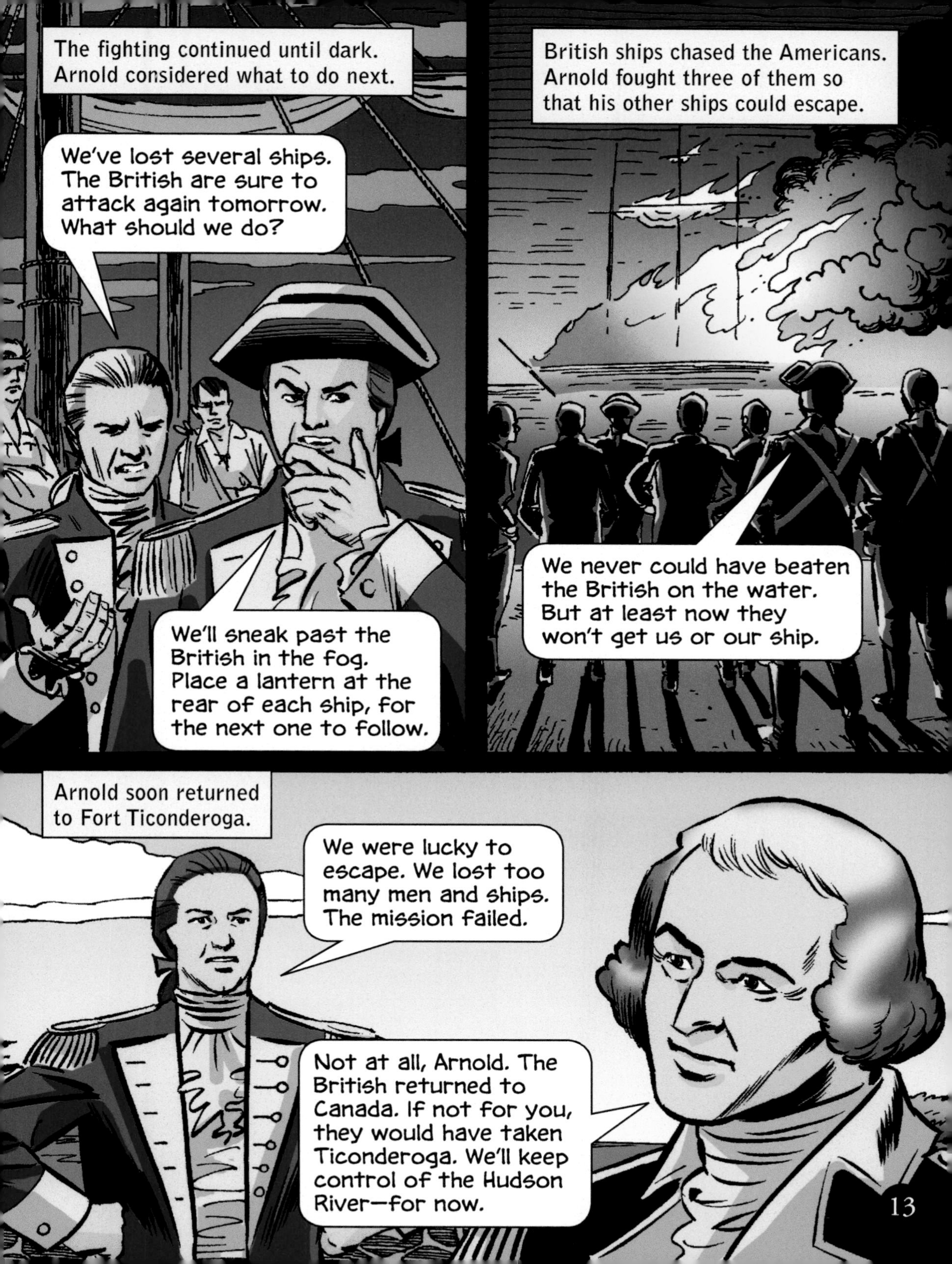
The fighting continued until dark. Arnold considered what to do next.
We've lost several ships. The British are sure to attack again tomorrow. What should we do?
We'll sneak past the British in the fog. Place a lantern at the rear of each ship, for the next one to follow.
British ships chased the Americans. Arnold fought three of them so that his other ships could escape.
We never could have beaten the British on the water. But at least now they won't get us or our ship.
Arnold soon returned to Fort Ticonderoga.
We were lucky to escape. We lost too many men and ships. The mission failed.
Not at all, Arnold. The British returned to Canada. If not for you, they would have taken Ticonderoga. We'll keep control of the Hudson River—for now.

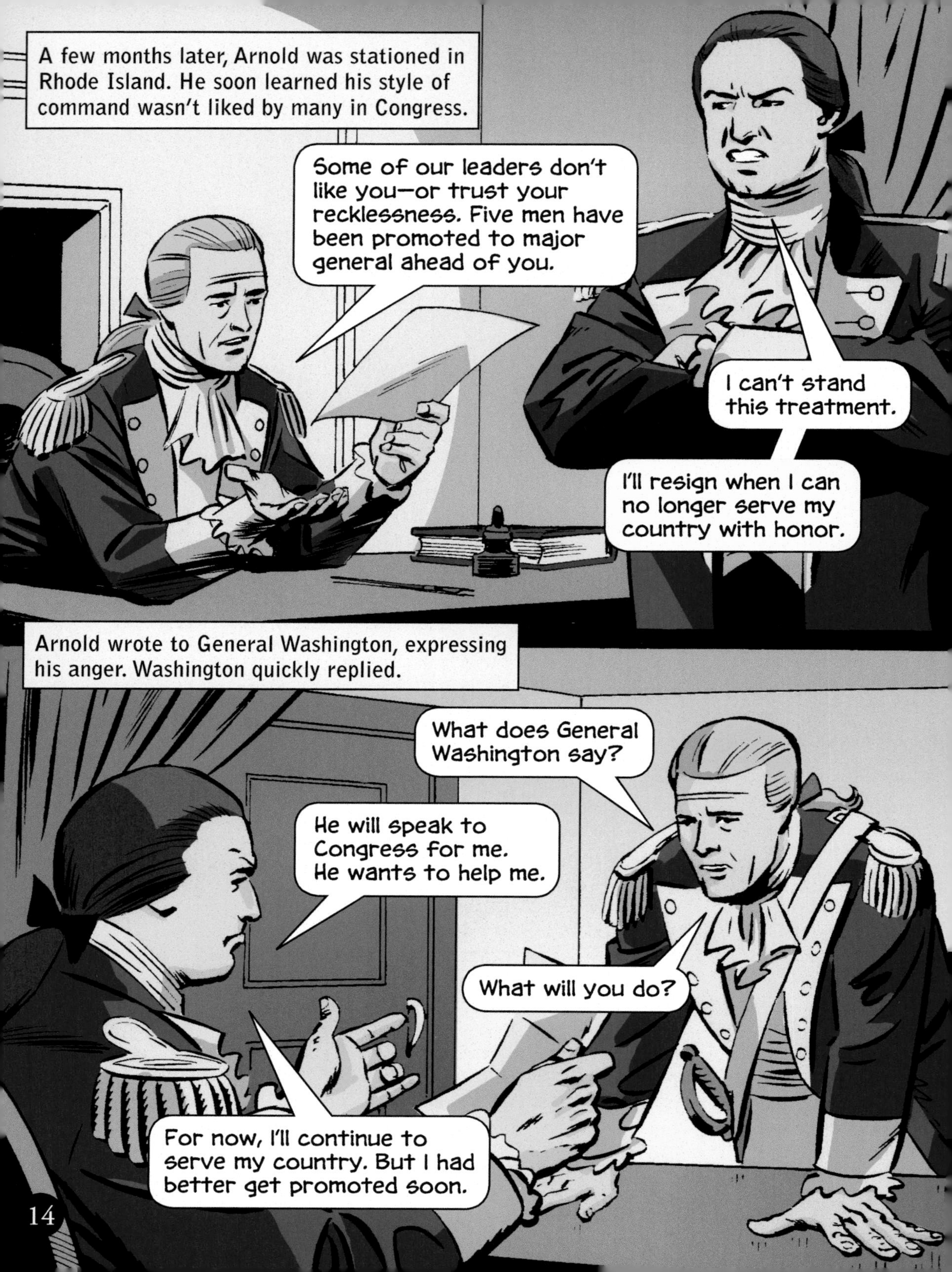

A few months later, Arnold was stationed in Rhode Island. He soon learned his style of command wasn't liked by many in Congress.
Some of our leaders don't like you—or trust your recklessness. Five men have been promoted to major general ahead of you.
I can't stand this treatment.
I'll resign when I can no longer serve my country with honor.
Arnold wrote to General Washington, expressing his anger. Washington quickly replied.
What does General Washington say?
He will speak to Congress for me. He wants to help me.
What will you do?
For now, I'll continue to serve my country. But I had better get promoted soon.

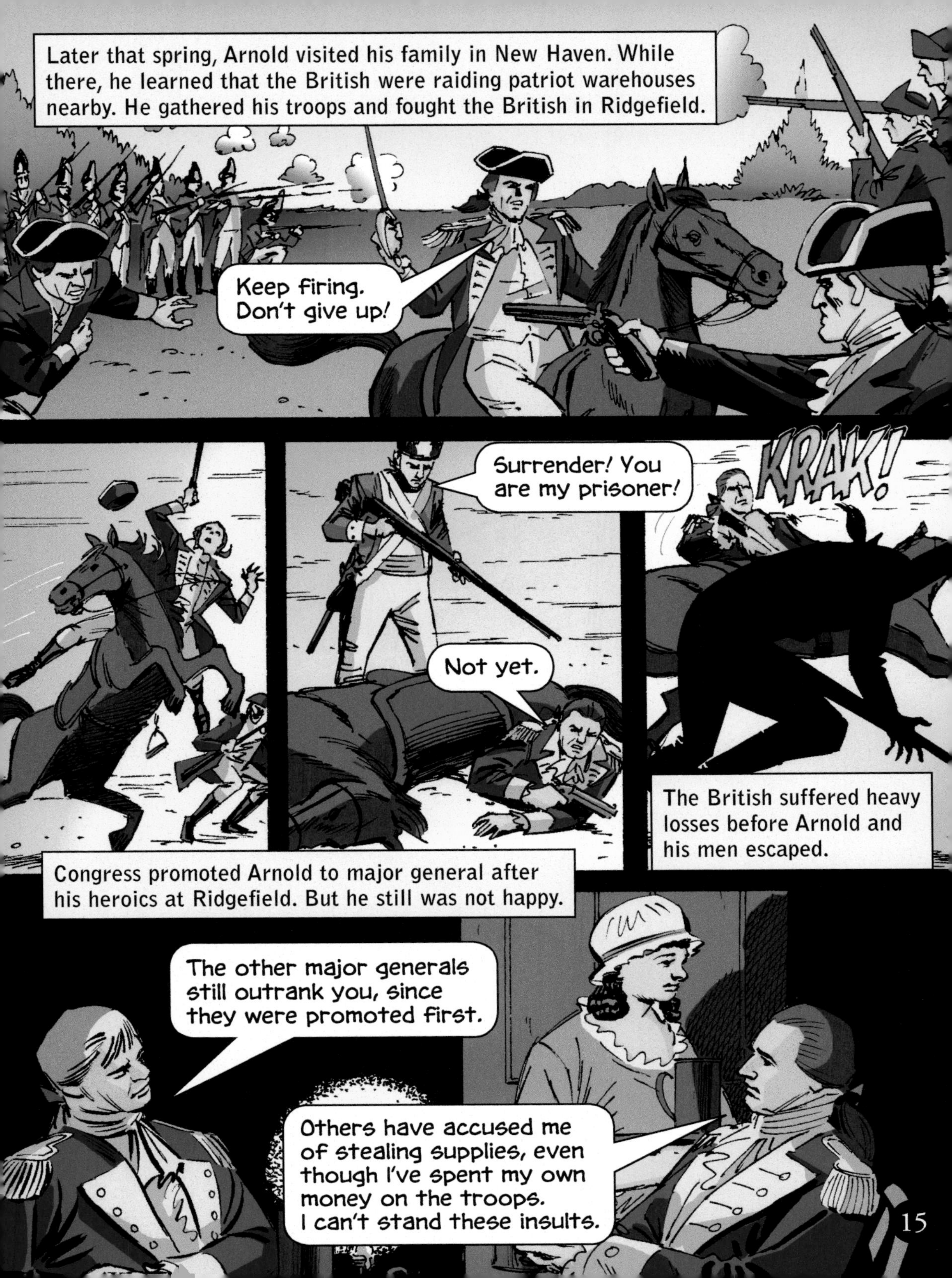
Later that spring, Arnold visited his family in New Haven. While there, he learned that the British were raiding patriot warehouses nearby. He gathered his troops and fought the British in Ridgefield.
Keep firing. Don't give up!
Surrender! You are my prisoner!
Not yet.
KRAK!
The British suffered heavy losses before Arnold and his men escaped.
Congress promoted Arnold to major general after his heroics at Ridgefield. But he still was not happy.
The other major generals still outrank you, since they were promoted first.
Others have accused me of stealing supplies, even though I've spent my own money on the troops. I can't stand these insults.

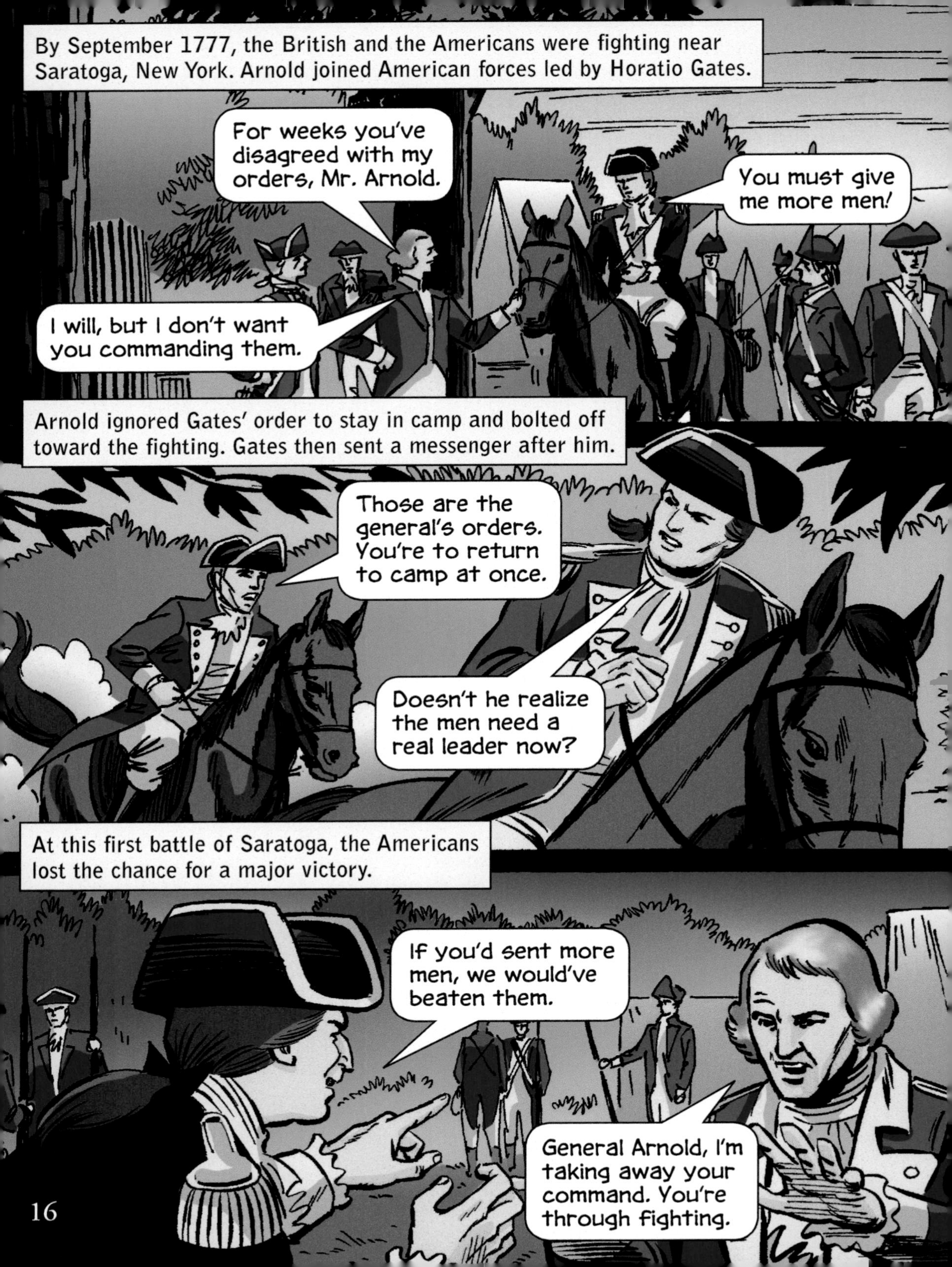
By September 1777, the British and the Americans were fighting near Saratoga, New York. Arnold joined American forces led by Horatio Gates.
For weeks you've disagreed with my orders, Mr. Arnold.
You must give me more men!
I will, but I don't want you commanding them.
Arnold ignored Gates' order to stay in camp and bolted off toward the fighting. Gates then sent a messenger after him.
Those are the general's orders. You're to return to camp at once.
Doesn't he realize the men need a real leader now?
At this first battle of Saratoga, the Americans lost the chance for a major victory.
If you'd sent more men, we would've beaten them.
General Arnold, I'm taking away your command. You're through fighting.

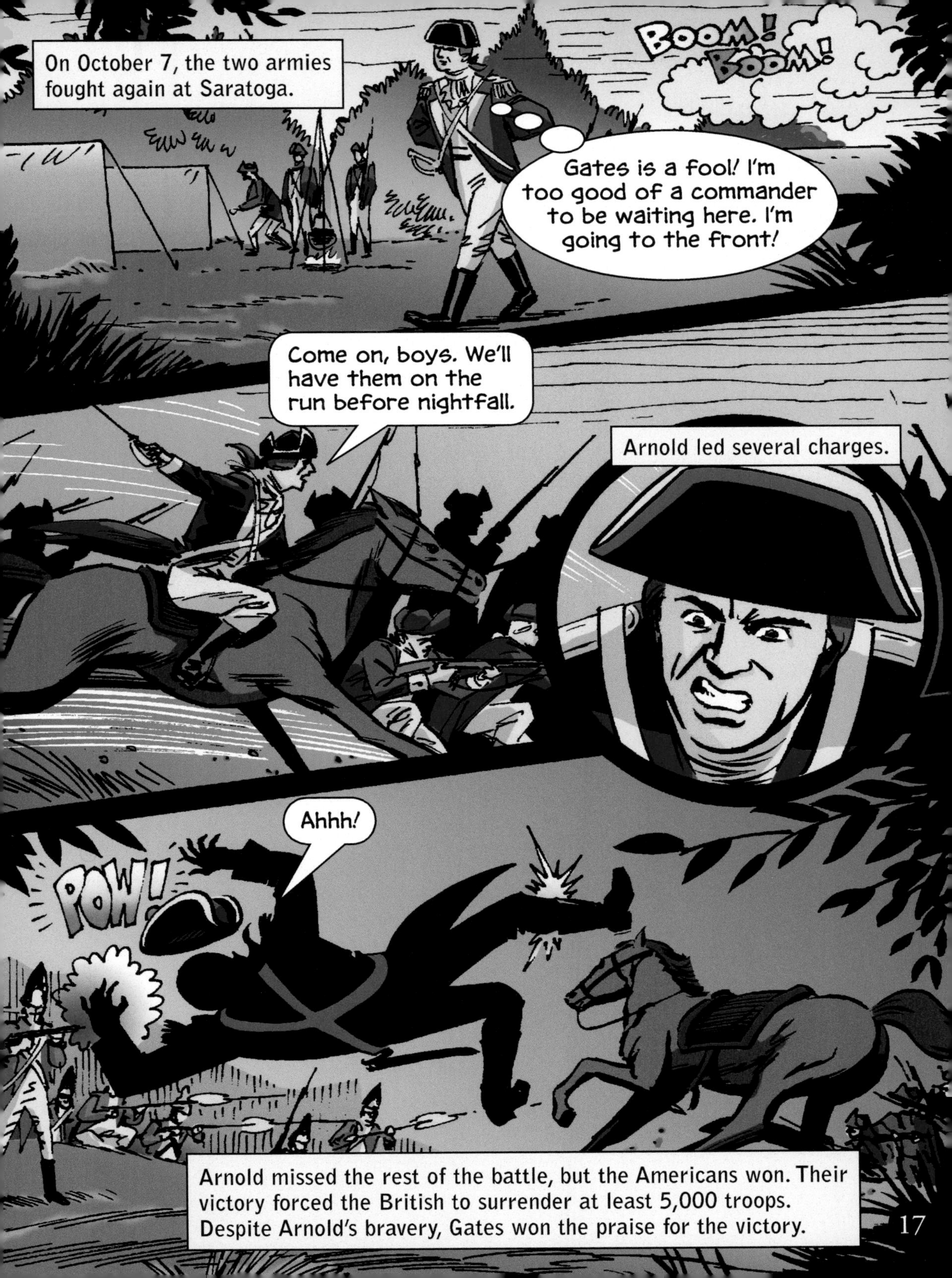
On October 7, the two armies fought again at Saratoga.
BOOM! BOOM!
Gates is a fool! I'm too good of a commander to be waiting here. I'm going to the front!
Come on, boys. We'll have them on the run before nightfall.
Arnold led several charges.
Ahhh!
POW!
Arnold missed the rest of the battle, but the Americans won. Their victory forced the British to surrender at least 5,000 troops. Despite Arnold's bravery, Gates won the praise for the victory.

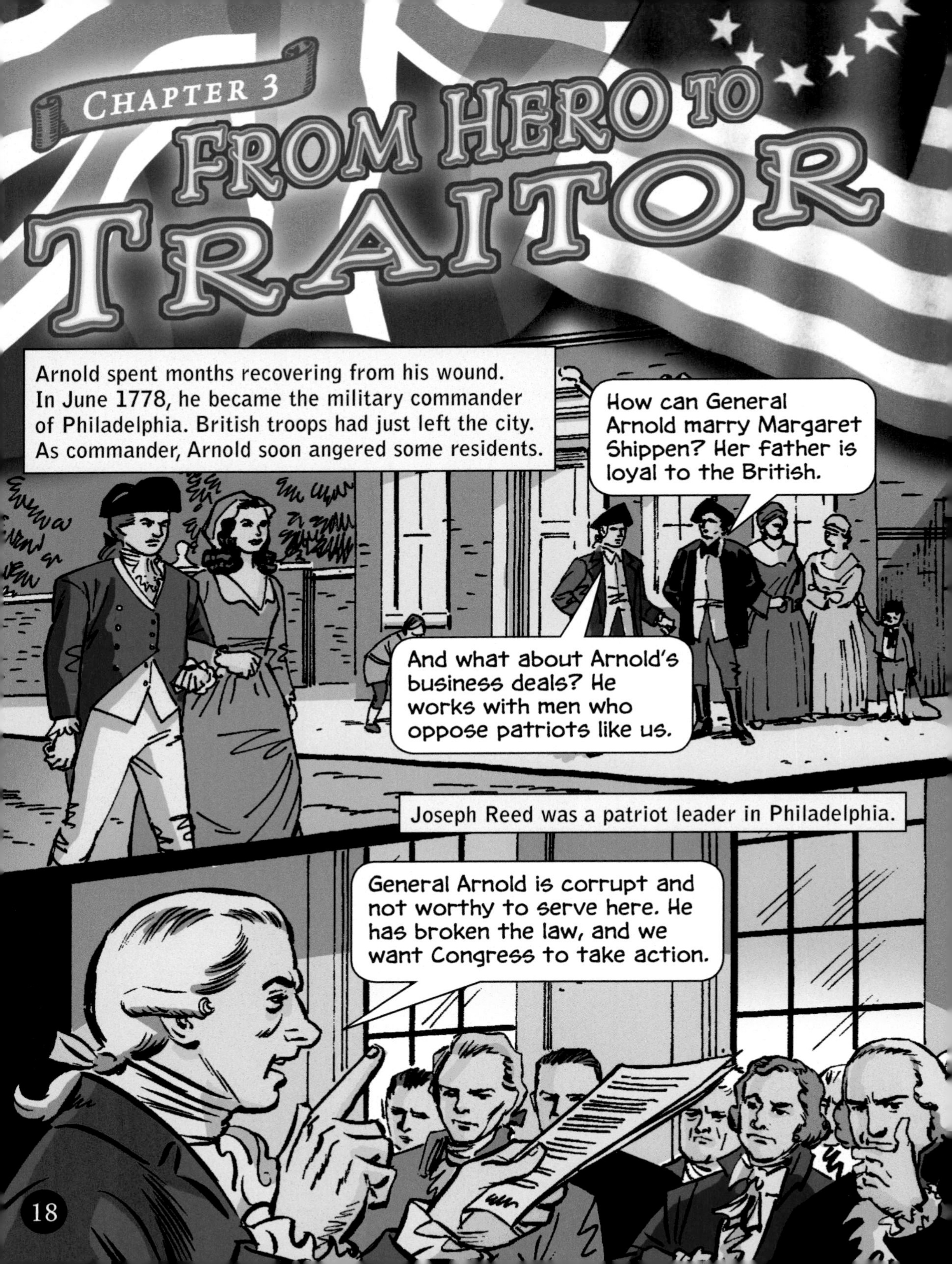
CHAPTER 3
FROM HERO TO TRAITOR
Arnold spent months recovering from his wound. In June 1778, he became the military commander of Philadelphia. British troops had just left the city. As commander, Arnold soon angered some residents.
How can General Arnold marry Margaret Shippen? Her father is loyal to the British.
And what about Arnold's business deals? He works with men who oppose patriots like us.
Joseph Reed was a patriot leader in Philadelphia.
General Arnold is corrupt and not worthy to serve here. He has broken the law, and we want Congress to take action.

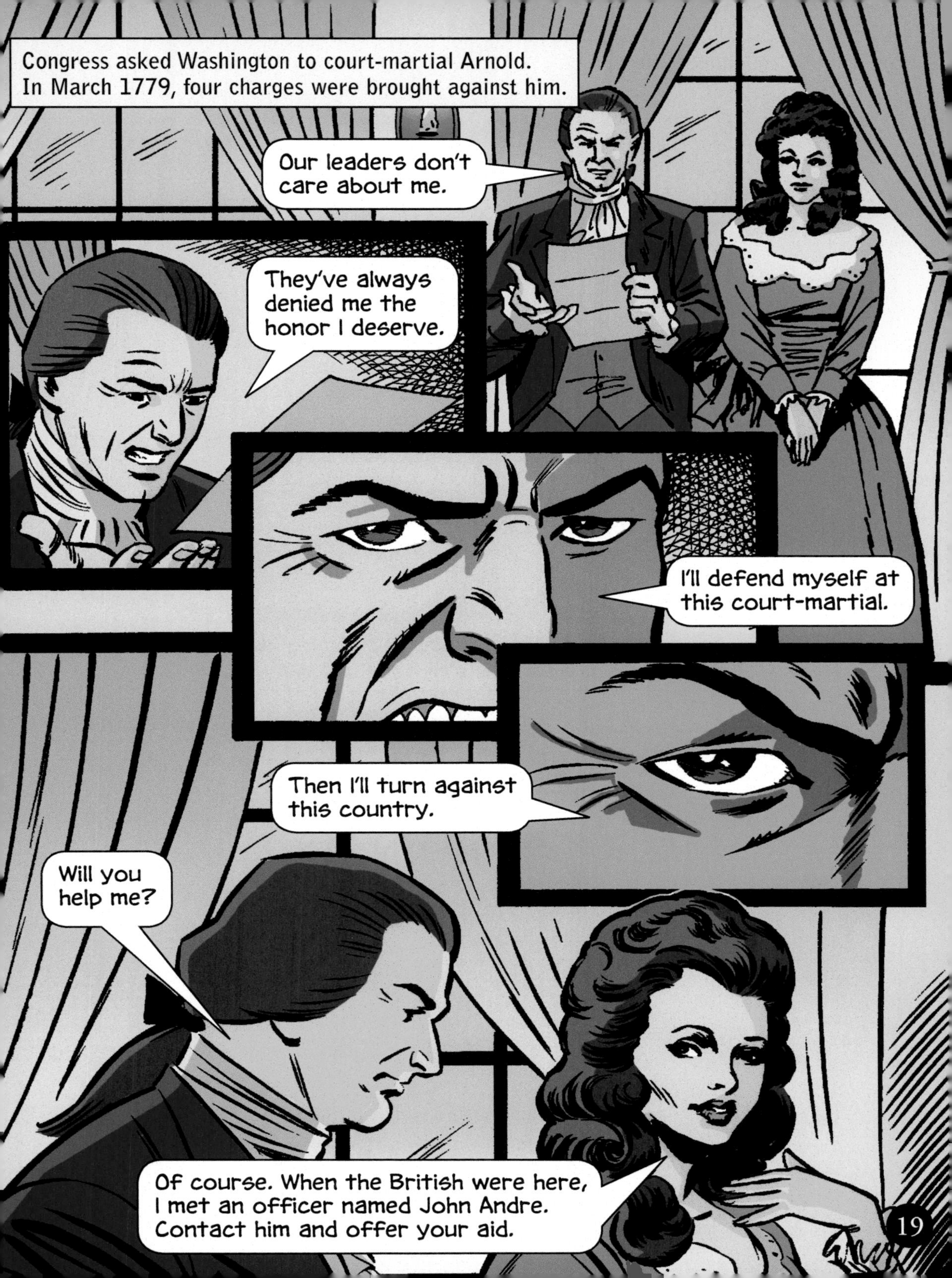

Congress asked Washington to court-martial Arnold. In March 1779, four charges were brought against him.
Our leaders don't care about me.
They've always denied me the honor I deserve.
I'll defend myself at this court-martial.
Then I'll turn against this country.
Will you help me?
Of course. When the British were here, I met an officer named John Andre. Contact him and offer your aid.

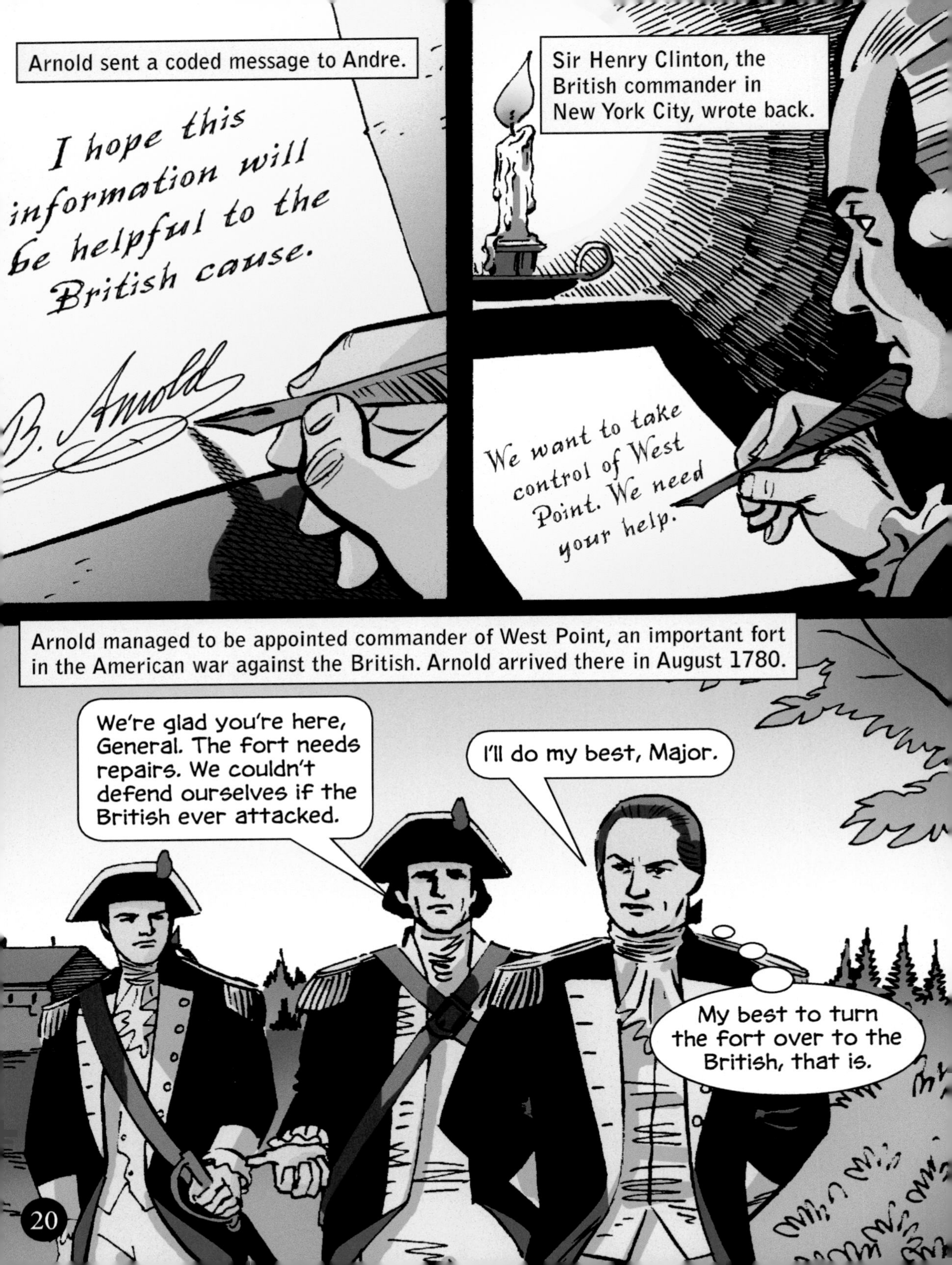

Arnold sent a coded message to Andre.
I hope this information will be helpful to the British cause.
B. Arnold
Sir Henry Clinton, the British commander in New York City, wrote back.
We want to take control of West Point. We need your help.
Arnold managed to be appointed commander of West Point, an important fort in the American war against the British. Arnold arrived there in August 1780.
We're glad you're here, General. The fort needs repairs. We couldn't defend ourselves if the British ever attacked.
I'll do my best, Major.
My best to turn the fort over to the British, that is.

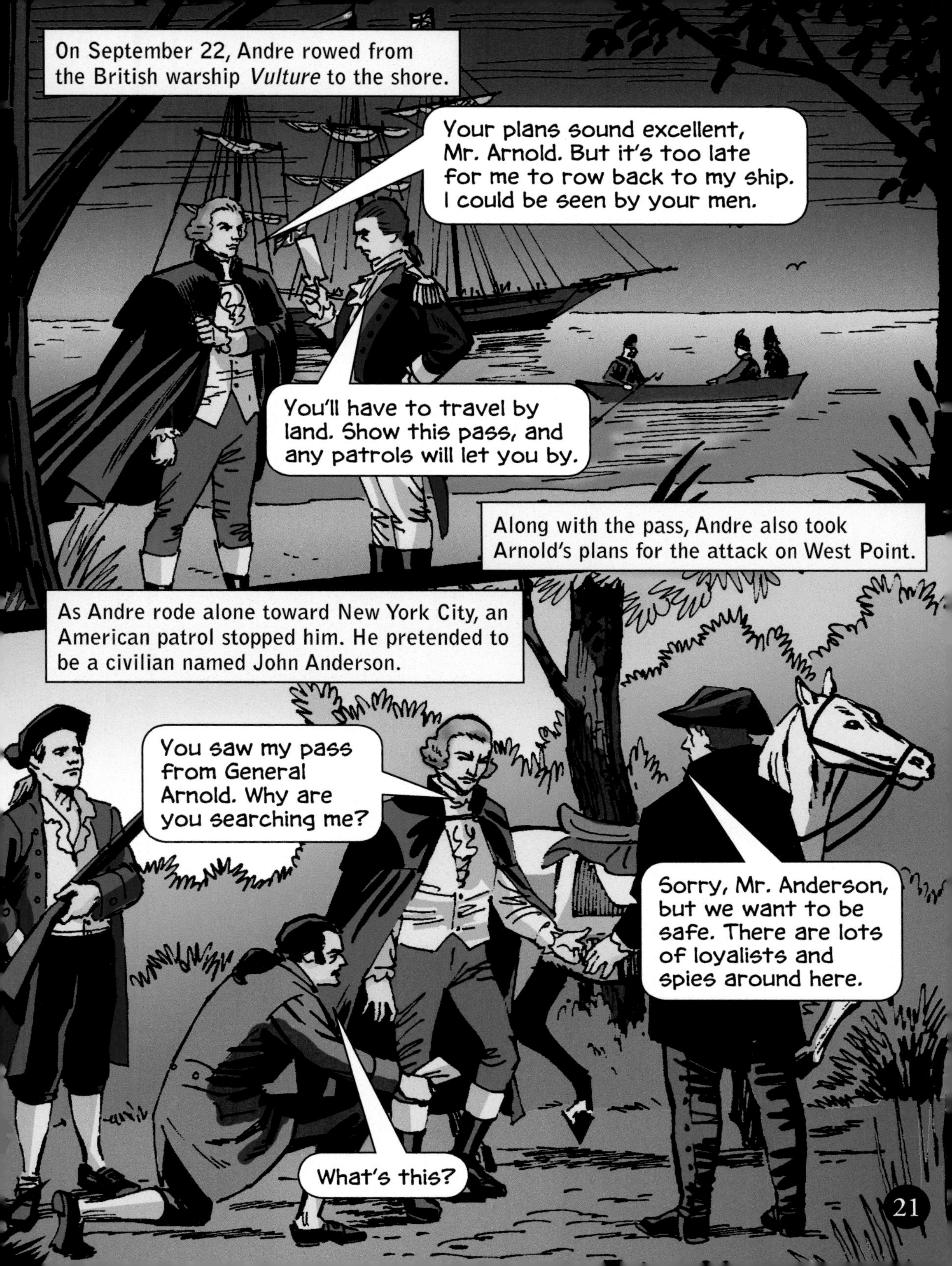
On September 22, Andre rowed from the British warship *Vulture* to the shore.
Your plans sound excellent, Mr. Arnold. But it's too late for me to row back to my ship. I could be seen by your men.
You'll have to travel by land. Show this pass, and any patrols will let you by.
Along with the pass, Andre also took Arnold's plans for the attack on West Point.
As Andre rode alone toward New York City, an American patrol stopped him. He pretended to be a civilian named John Anderson.
You saw my pass from General Arnold. Why are you searching me?
Sorry, Mr. Anderson, but we want to be safe. There are lots of loyalists and spies around here.
What's this?

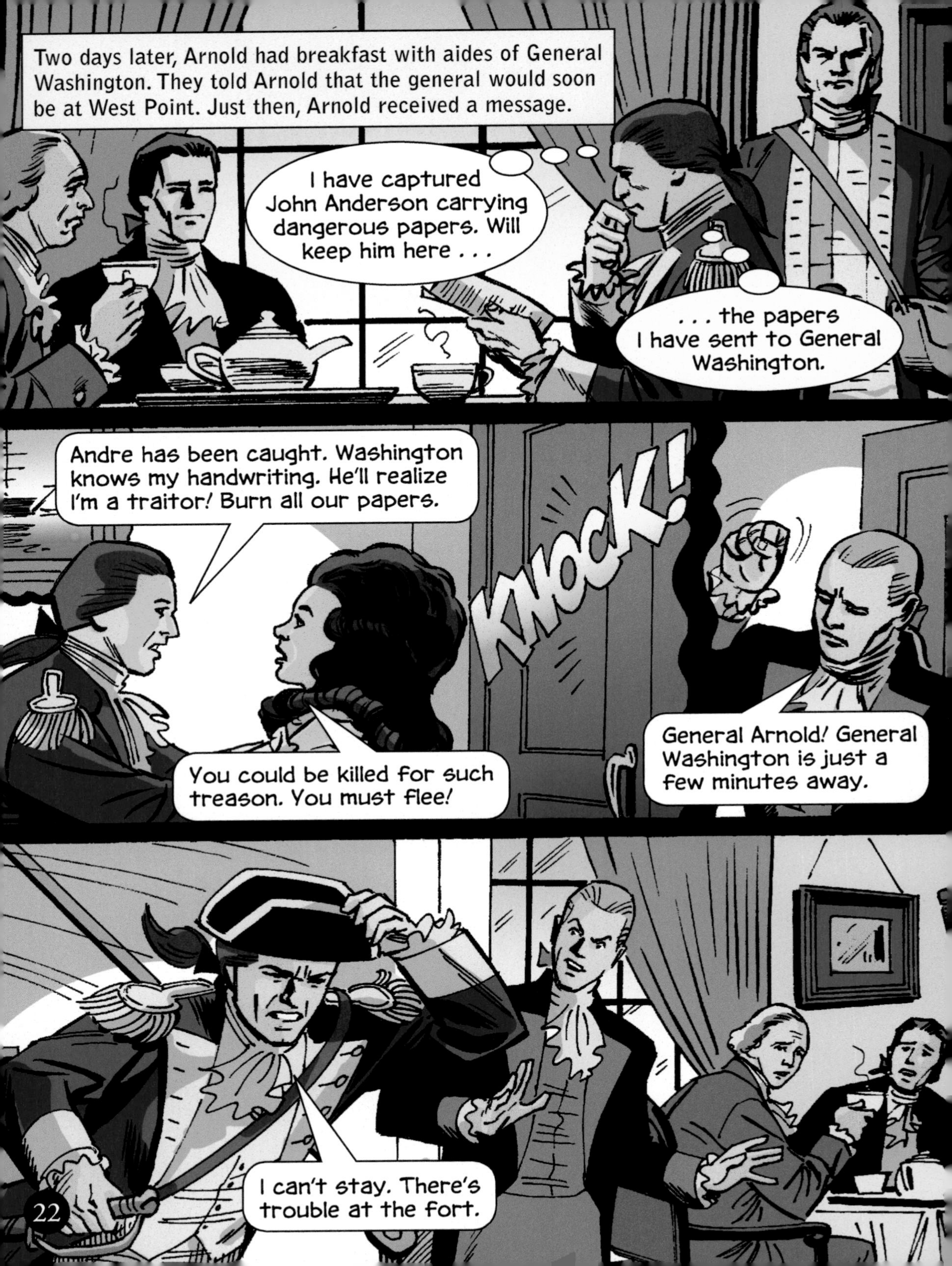

Two days later, Arnold had breakfast with aides of General Washington. They told Arnold that the general would soon be at West Point. Just then, Arnold received a message.
I have captured John Anderson carrying dangerous papers. Will keep him here . . .
. . . the papers I have sent to General Washington.
Andre has been caught. Washington knows my handwriting. He'll realize I'm a traitor! Burn all our papers.
You could be killed for such treason. You must flee!
KNOCK!
General Arnold! General Washington is just a few minutes away.
I can't stay. There's trouble at the fort.

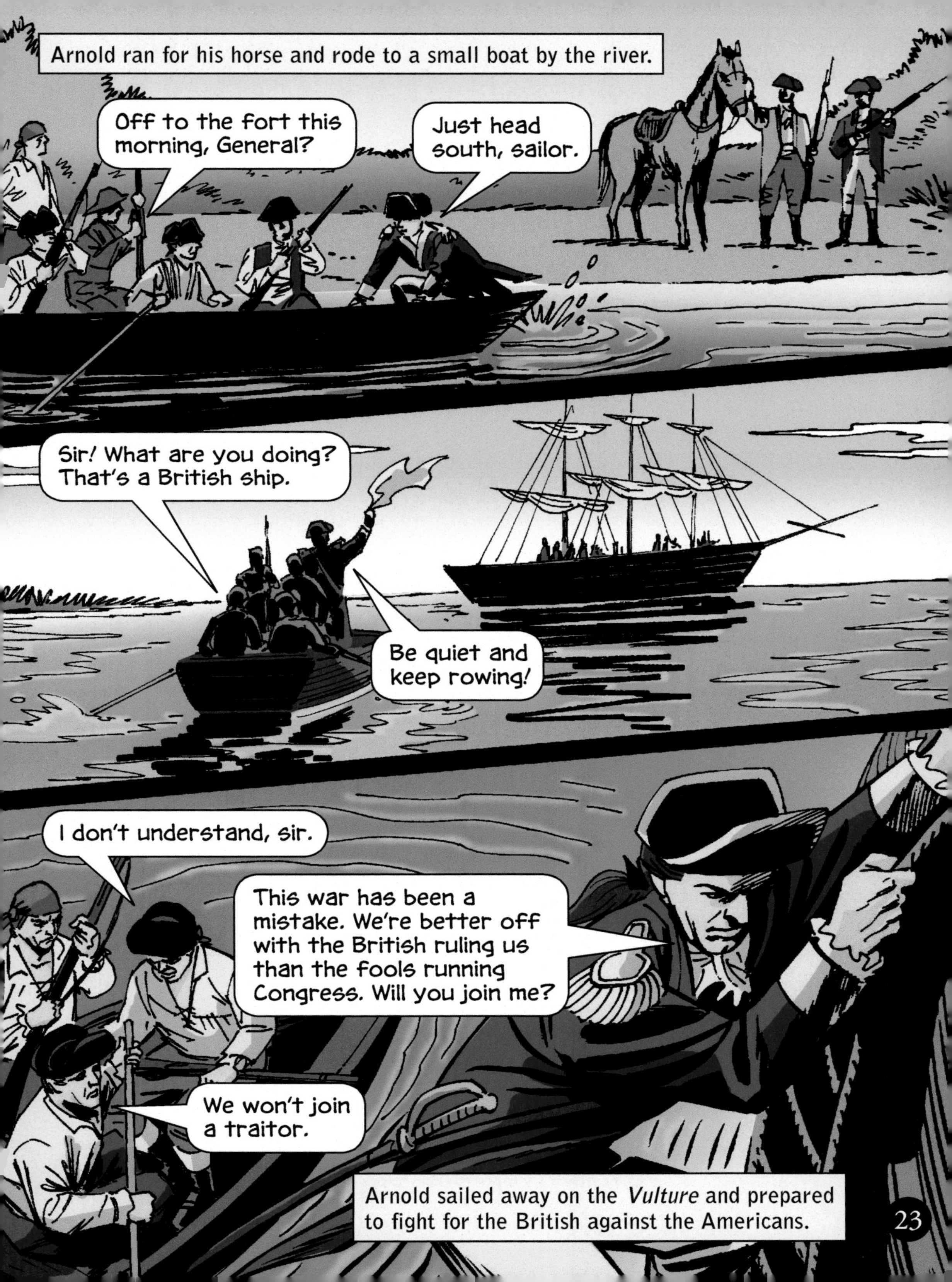
Arnold ran for his horse and rode to a small boat by the river.
Off to the fort this morning, General?
Just head south, sailor.
Sir! What are you doing? That's a British ship.
Be quiet and keep rowing!
I don't understand, sir.
This war has been a mistake. We're better off with the British ruling us than the fools running Congress. Will you join me?
We won't join a traitor.
Arnold sailed away on the *Vulture* and prepared to fight for the British against the Americans.

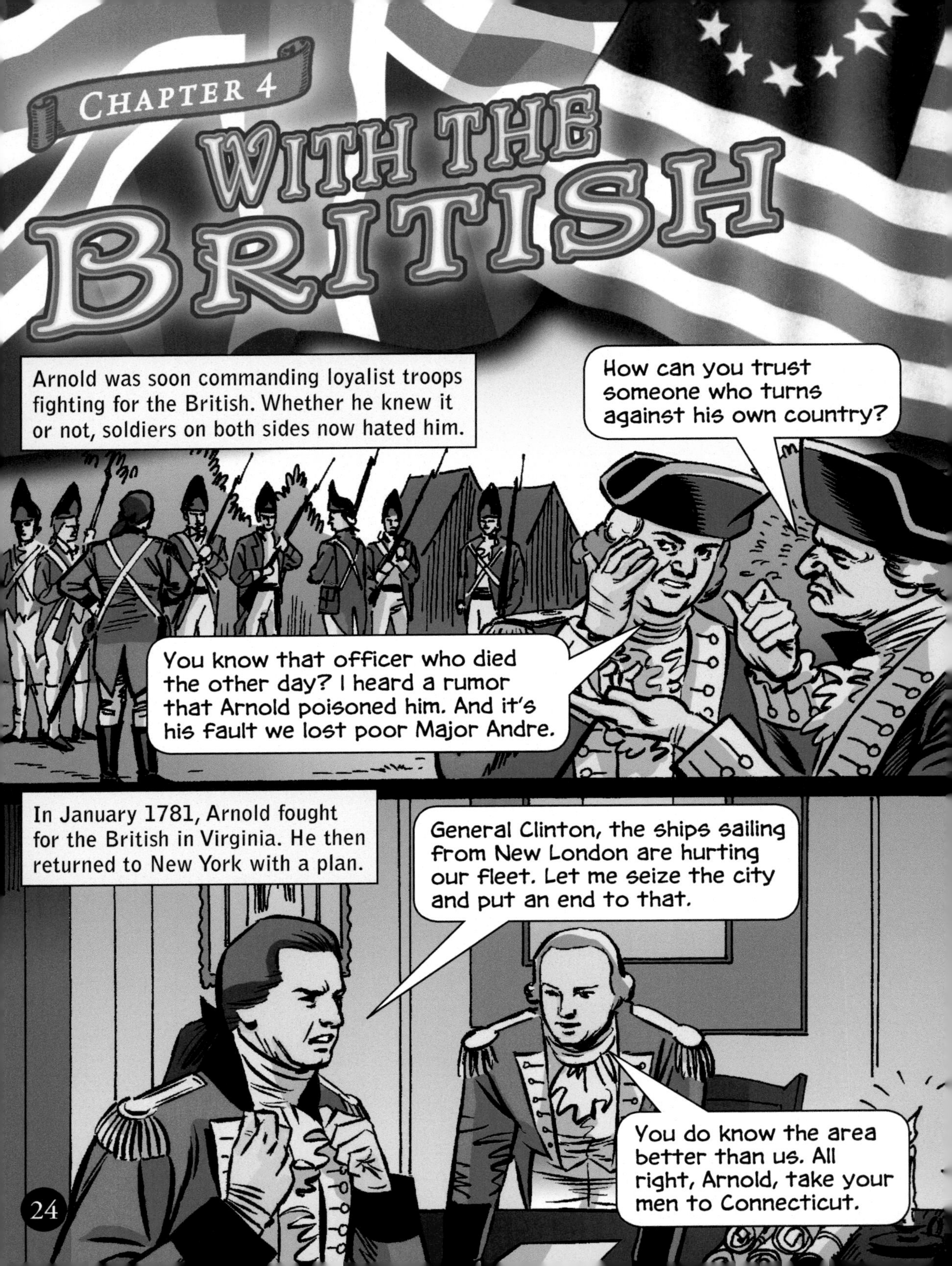
CHAPTER 4
WITH THE BRITISH
Arnold was soon commanding loyalist troops fighting for the British. Whether he knew it or not, soldiers on both sides now hated him.
How can you trust someone who turns against his own country?
You know that officer who died the other day? I heard a rumor that Arnold poisoned him. And it's his fault we lost poor Major Andre.
In January 1781, Arnold fought for the British in Virginia. He then returned to New York with a plan.
General Clinton, the ships sailing from New London are hurting our fleet. Let me seize the city and put an end to that.
You do know the area better than us. All right, Arnold, take your men to Connecticut.

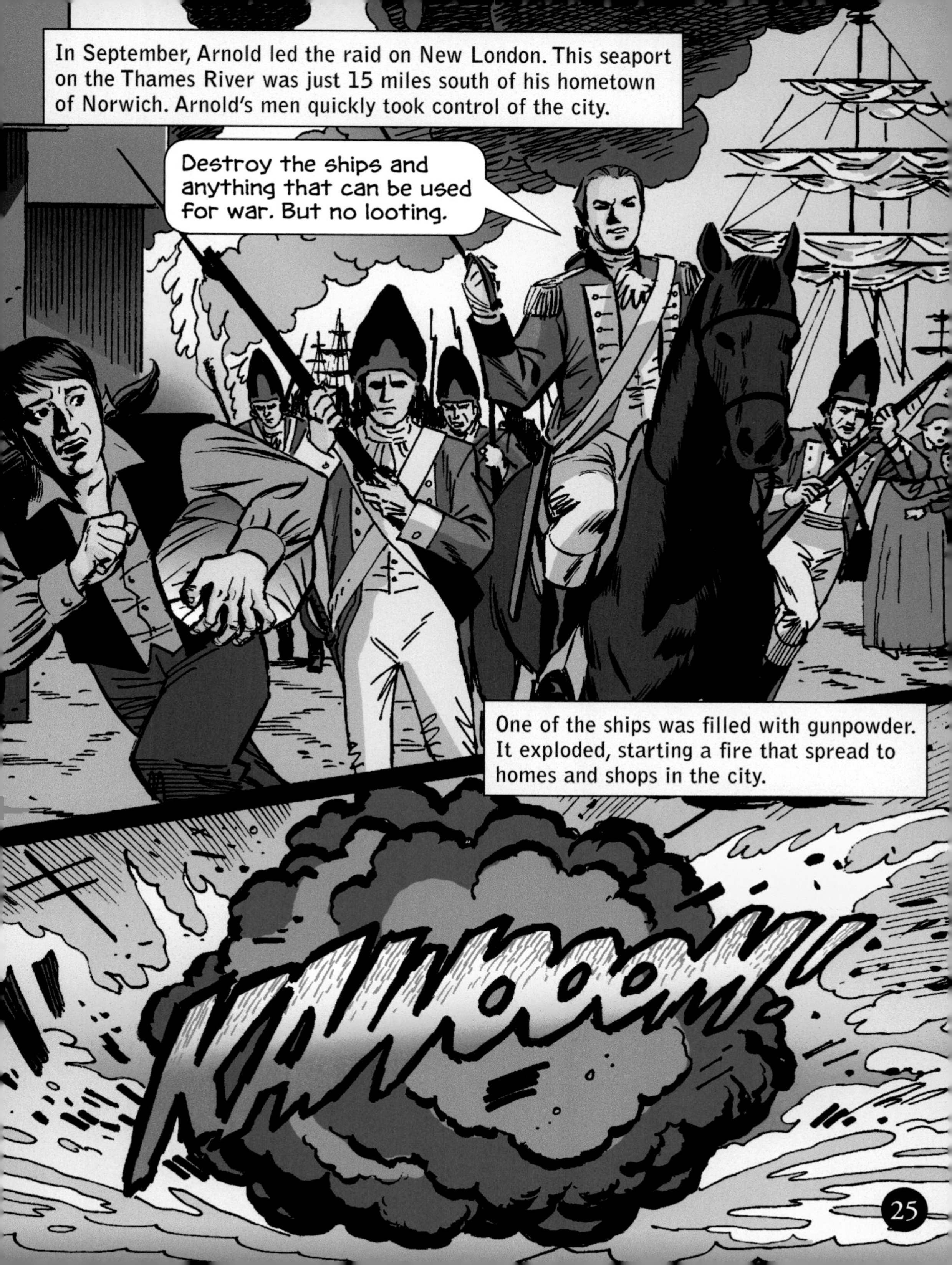
In September, Arnold led the raid on New London. This seaport on the Thames River was just 15 miles south of his hometown of Norwich. Arnold's men quickly took control of the city.
Destroy the ships and anything that can be used for war. But no looting.
One of the ships was filled with gunpowder. It exploded, starting a fire that spread to homes and shops in the city.
KA-BOOM!

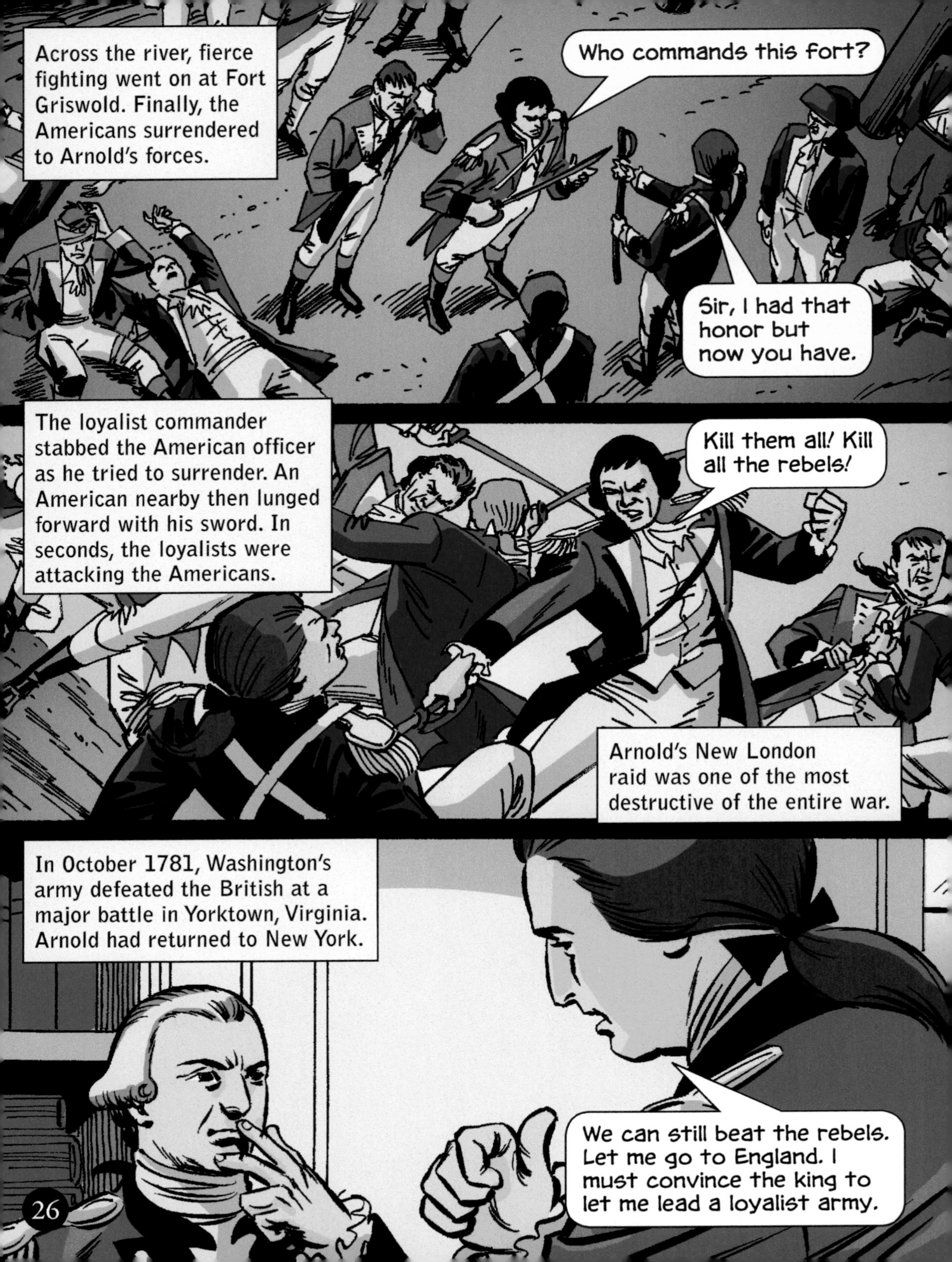
Across the river, fierce fighting went on at Fort Griswold. Finally, the Americans surrendered to Arnold's forces.
Who commands this fort?
Sir, I had that honor but now you have.
The loyalist commander stabbed the American officer as he tried to surrender. An American nearby then lunged forward with his sword. In seconds, the loyalists were attacking the Americans.
Kill them all! Kill all the rebels!
Arnold's New London raid was one of the most destructive of the entire war.
In October 1781, Washington's army defeated the British at a major battle in Yorktown, Virginia. Arnold had returned to New York.
We can still beat the rebels. Let me go to England. I must convince the king to let me lead a loyalist army.

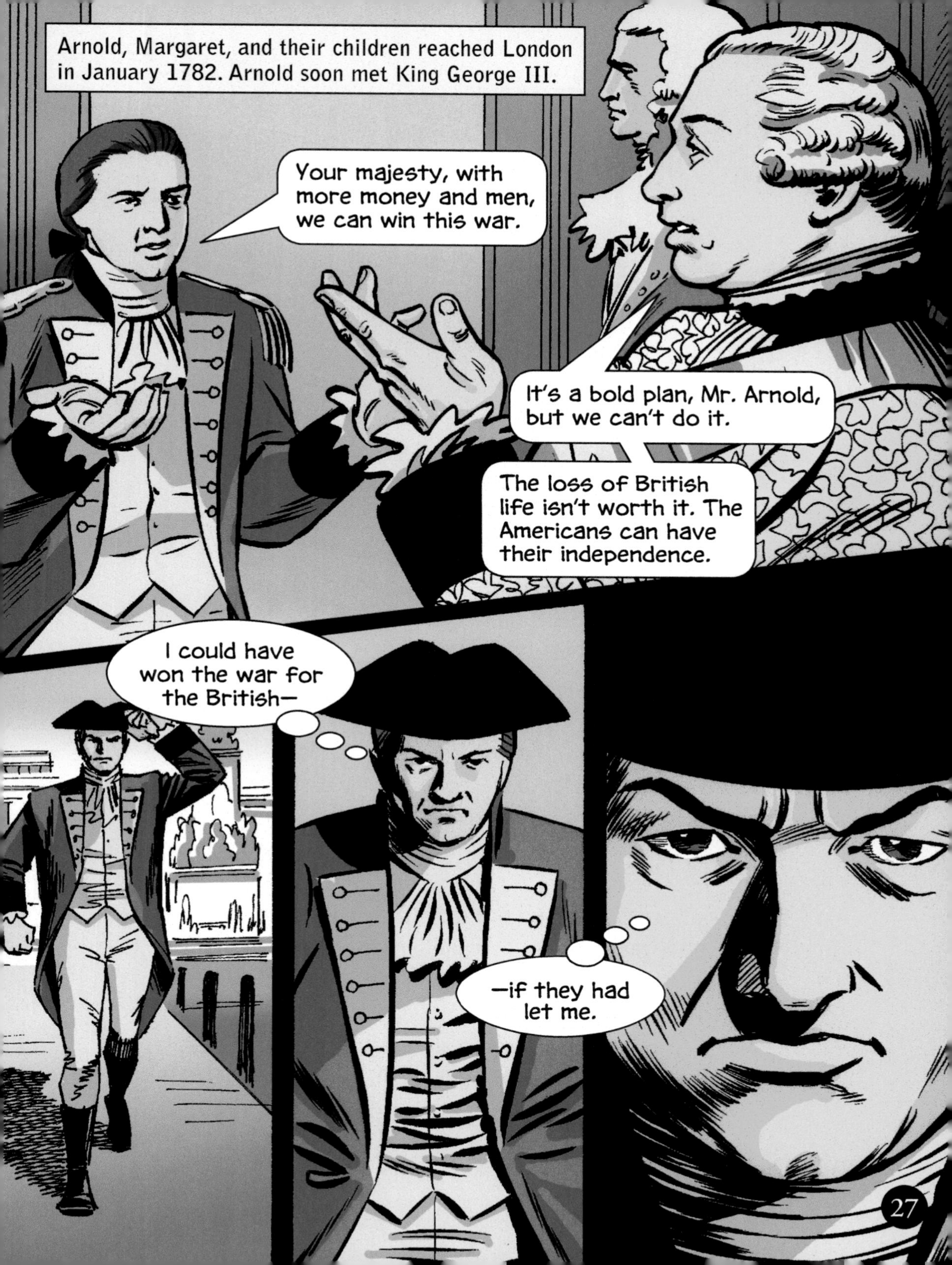

Arnold, Margaret, and their children reached London in January 1782. Arnold soon met King George III.
Your majesty, with more money and men, we can win this war.
It's a bold plan, Mr. Arnold, but we can't do it.
The loss of British life isn't worth it. The Americans can have their independence.
I could have won the war for the British—
—if they had let me.

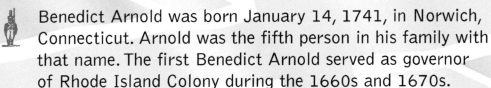

MORE ABOUT BENEDICT ARNOLD

Benedict Arnold was born January 14, 1741, in Norwich, Connecticut. Arnold was the fifth person in his family with that name. The first Benedict Arnold served as governor of Rhode Island Colony during the 1660s and 1670s.

Arnold has sometimes been called the "Father of the American Navy" because of the fleet he built on Lake Champlain in 1776.

At his court-martial in 1779, Arnold argued he was innocent of the major charges against him. The court found that he did not break the law, but he had twice acted improperly. For his punishment, Arnold received a public scolding from General Washington.

After his arrest, Major John Andre was hanged as a spy. Andre had been a popular officer, and many British soldiers and citizens blamed Arnold for his death.

The U.S. Constitution is the document that outlines the form of government used in the United States. The only crime defined in the Constitution is treason. It is defined as a citizen waging war against the United States or aiding an enemy during wartime.

28

For turning over West Point, Arnold wanted the British to pay him a fee that would be equal to $1.6 million today. He eventually received less than half of that, though the British also paid him a salary every year for the rest of his life.

Some patriot soldiers angered by Arnold's treason hoped to kill or capture him in battle. Many claimed that they wanted to cut off the leg he wounded at Quebec and Saratoga. They would then give his leg the kind of burial given to a military hero. They wanted to hang the remainder of Arnold's body as a traitor. A monument on the battlefield at Saratoga shows Arnold's leg, but it does not mention him by name.

After the American Revolution ended in 1783, Arnold and his family divided their time between Canada and England. Arnold rebuilt his trading business. Arnold died in London on June 14, 1801.

Today, many Americans still call someone who commits treason a "Benedict Arnold."

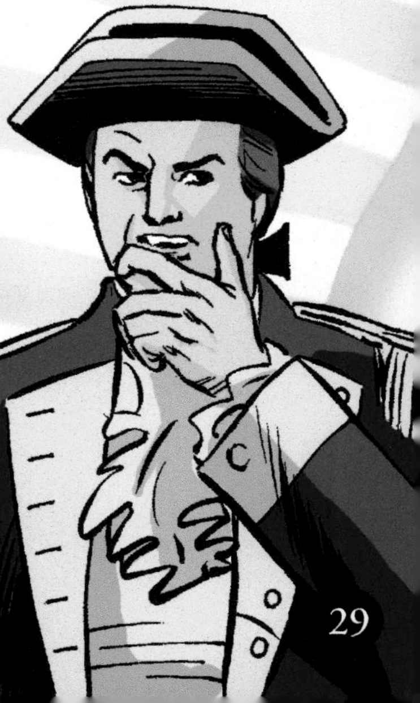

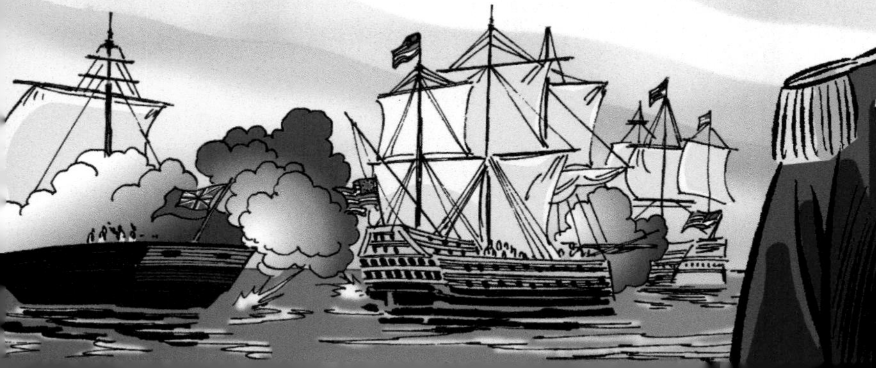

GLOSSARY

brigadier (brig-uh-DEER)—the lowest of several levels within the military rank of general

civilian (si-VIL-yuhn)—a person who is not in the military

Continental Congress (KON-tuh-nen-tuhl KONG-griss)—leaders from the 13 original American Colonies that served as the American government from 1774 to 1789

court-martial (KORT-MAR-shuhl)—a military trial

loyalist (LOI-uh-list)—a colonist who was loyal to Great Britain during the Revolutionary War

patriot (PAY-tree-uht)—a person who sided with the colonies during the Revolutionary War

smuggle (SMUHG-uhl)—to sneak something in or out of a country illegally

treason (TREE-zuhn)—the act of turning against one's country

INTERNET SITES

FactHound offers a safe, fun way to find Internet sites related to this book. All of the sites on FactHound have been researched by our staff.

Here's how:
1. Visit *www.facthound.com*
2. Choose your grade level.
3. Type in this book ID **0736868542** for age-appropriate sites. You may also browse subjects by clicking on letters, or by clicking on pictures and words.
4. Click on the **Fetch It** button.

FactHound will fetch the best sites for you!

READ MORE

Anderson, Dale. *Leaders of the American Revolution.* World Almanac Library of the American Revolution. Milwaukee: World Almanac Library, 2006.

Bobrick, Benson. *Fight for Freedom: The American Revolutionary War.* New York: Atheneum Books for Young Readers, 2004.

Price Hossell, Karen. *Benedict Arnold.* American War Biographies. Chicago: Heinemann, 2004.

Sonneborn, Liz. *Benedict Arnold: Hero and Traitor.* Leaders of the American Revolution. Philadelphia: Chelsea House, 2006.

BIBLIOGRAPHY

Arnold, Isaac N. *The Life of Benedict Arnold: His Patriotism and His Treason.* Chicago: Jansen, McClurg and Company, 1880.

Brandt, Clare. *The Man in the Mirror: A Life of Benedict Arnold.* New York: Random House, 1994.

Fleming, Thomas. *Liberty! The American Revolution.* New York: Viking, 1997.

Randall, Willard Sterne. *Benedict Arnold: Patriot and Traitor.* New York: Morrow, 1990.

INDEX